JUDAISM DESPITE CHRISTIANITY

JUDAISM DESPITE CHRISTIANITY

The "Letters on Christianity and Judaism"
between Eugen Rosenstock-Huessy and Franz Rosenzweig

Edited by Eugen Rosenstock-Huessy

SCHOCKEN BOOKS · NEW YORK

ACKNOWLEDGEMENTS

Sincere thanks are due a number of people who have helped to make the present work possible.

Franz Rosenzweig's widow, now Mrs. Edith Scheinmann of Berlin, Germany, graciously gave permission for her late husband's letters to be published in English translation.

Professor Dorothy Emmet, of the University of Manchester, generously donated a sympathetic and astute translation of the correspondence. Her work, based on the letters printed in an appendix to Franz Rosenzweig's *Briefe*, has been amended in many places, but most of these revisions are relatively minor ones, and the reader should understand that the translation as printed is essentially hers.

The University of Chicago Press and the editors of *The Journal of Religion* granted permission to reprint the essays by Miss Emmet and Professor Alexander Altmann, of Brandeis University. Professor Altmann was kind enough to make several valuable additions to his essay.

Finally, I am deeply grateful to Professor Harold Stahmer, of Barnard College, for his original contribution to the present volume, and to Mr. Clinton Gardner for his advice and counsel at critical stages in the preparation of the manuscript.

Eugen Rosenstock-Huessy

Four Wells
Norwich, Vermont 05055
October, 1968

TABLE OF CONTENTS

JUDAISM DESPITE CHRISTIANITY

INTRODUCTION

I

This unusual collection of letters and essays spans half a century of spiritual and cultural disintegration and concurrent attempts at renewal and reform. In Rosenstock-Huessy's words, the "facts of life" during this period include, among other things, "the murder of six million Jews, two world wars, an ecumenical council, a panarabic upheaval," and "700 million Chinese entering the orbit of Christendom."[1] The style of the work is distinguished on a number of counts. For one thing, this is not a "textbook" of the sort that academic people and their students are wont to expect and that the former, all too often, spend a lifetime writing; this work is, indeed, an anti-textbook. The issues and problems treated are not sorted out neatly according to the abstract, neutral, timeless categories and concepts that the authors of textbooks—and, in fact, the authors of most scholarly works—seem to find so satisfying. Rosenstock-Huessy came to the realization very early in life that history is a matter of passion—that history is something in which persons and nations are deeply involved, rather than something merely to be contemplated and speculated about—and Rosenzweig came to share this conviction. As Rosenstock-Huessy put it in the "post-war preface" to his *Out of Revolution: The Autobiography of Western Man* (1938): "Our passions give

---

[1] From a personal letter, Sept. 27, 1966.

life to the world, our collective passions constitute the history of mankind."[2] Further: "A different type of man and woman is produced by stimulating or repressing different potential passions; and any special society is based on a peculiar selection in admitting or negating the innumerable desires of our hearts . . . . When a nation, or [an] individual, declines the experiences that present themselves to passionate hearts only, they are automatically turned out from the realm of history."[3]

The reader must be warned, then, that the customary distance from subject matter—that sense of "objectivity" and "neutrality" that most academic people have been conditioned to expect and even to demand—is nowhere to be found in the "Letters on Judaism and Christianity" that comprise the greater part of the volume. The usual subject/object antinomies, which preclude personal involvement, feelings of shame, embarrassment, and hope, seemed to Rosenstock, at least as early as 1910, to be a reflection of the irresponsibly "neutral" academic mentality that was eventually to contribute significantly, albeit unintentionally, to calamities such as Hitler's rise to power, to the murder of those six million Jews, and to the moral and spiritual morass that present generations in the West are experiencing and that subsequent generations will yet be sacrificed for.[4]

As Rosenstock-Huessy remarked on one occasion: "It is part of the whole naïveté of the educated that German academics do not know how in 1933 they forfeited their status as participants in the *logos*; they do not know that only through the [courage and deeds of the] resistance fighters [in Hitler's Germany], and not through knowledge or erudition, do [scholars] have the right to continue their research or teaching in the German language." In the same essay—by Mrs. Sabine Leibholz, twin sister of the

[2] Eugen Rosenstock-Huessy, *Out of Revolution* (New York: William Morrow & Company, 1938), p. 3. For a fuller discussion of these themes cf. Page Smith, *The Historian and History* (New York: Alfred A. Knopf, 1964), pp. 95–96; Carl J. Friedrich (ed.) *Revolution* (New York: Atherton, 1966) pp. v–vi, 122–135.

[3] *Out of Revolution*, p. 4.

[4] Cf. Professor Altmann's article, this volume, pp. 26–48.

Christian martyr Dietrich Bonhoeffer—Rosenstock is quoted as saying, to a German audience: "The position you take with regard to the 20th July, 1944 determines whether you as Germans can have forefathers. Thus history is made to live again through evocation, and we must decide as from now what of our past history belongs to the future. [The] evoking of history is not only a matter for parents or commanding statesmen and leaders of spiritual life, but [also] concerns us teachers."[5] Elsewhere Rosenstock described the complete breakdown of the German language between 1933 and 1939 as "one of the speediest and most radical events of all times in the field of mind and speech." This experience more than any other confirmed his conviction that language, that *speech*, is the "science of this life blood of society and should . . . be exalted to the rank of social research."[6]

The setting for the "Letters on Judaism and Christianity" is, therefore, to use Father Walter J. Ong's phrase, an "oral and aural" one.[7] The styles of Rosenstock-Huessy and Rosenzweig, like those of Bonhoeffer and Camus, reflect an overwhelming sense of involvement in history. The letters, as indeed the other writings of both correspondents, are unusually personal and autobiographical, seeming to be almost involuntary responses wrung

[5] On July 20, 1944 an unsuccessful attempt was made on Hitler's life. Several of Hitler's staff were killed in the bomb plot and many others were subsequently executed by Hitler. Sabine Leibholz, "Eugen Rosenstock-Huessy and Dietrich Bonhoeffer—Two Witnesses to the Change in Our Time," *Universitas*, 8 (1966) 3, pp. 282–83, 286.

[6] Eugen Rosenstock-Huessy, "In Defense of the Grammatical Method" (1955). (Privately printed), p. 1. In the same essay he writes, "The circulation of articulated speech is the life blood of society. *Through speech, society sustains its time and space axes.* . . . When speech is recognized as curing society from the ills of disharmony and discontinuity in time and space, grammar is the most obvious organon for the teachings on society . . . . A science is sought by which we may diagnose the power, vitality, unanimity and prosperity of the life blood of society, of speech, language, literature . . . . Our method represents *remedial* linguistics . . ." p. 5.

[7] Ong, Father Walter J., *The Presence of the Word* (New Haven & London: Yale University Press, 1967). The epigraph to this work, translated (by Father Ong) from the second volume of Rosenstock-Huessy's *Soziologie*, reads: "Experiences of the first order, of the first rank, are not realized through the eye." (*Die Vollzahl der Zeiten* [1957], p. 33.)

out of men caught up in the kind of crisis situation in which neat distinctions between personal, spiritual, and historical perspectives are difficult or impossible to make—and are likely to be useless in any case. Quite accurately, the correspondence was cited by the late Fritz Kaufmann as a veritable model of "existential" dialogue. "True co-existenz," Kaufmann wrote, "in the consumation of face-to-face relationships is no less intensive and forceful for being unobtrusive, a model of non-violence." Such, he asserted, was the quality "alive in the highly charged controversy between Eugen Rosenstock-Huessy and Franz Rosenzweig in 1913 and 1916."[8] In retrospect, Rosenstock-Huessy made the following comment about their first significant encounter in 1913: "Much to their own surprise the two partners found themselves reluctantly put under the compulsion to face up to one another in a struggle with no quarter to be given or asked for ... For only in this last extremity, of a soul in self-defense, is there hope to realize the truth in the questions of life."[9]

Conversation, dialogue, speech set against speech was the method and medium wherein, at one stage in their lives, a Jew and a Christian discovered their respective identities and a common framework for answering their age's particular brand of spiritual agnosticism and academic and professional nihilism. Of the dialogical method Rosenzweig noted: ". . . . in the course of a dialogue he who happens to be listening also speaks, and he does not speak merely when he is actually uttering words, not even mainly when he is uttering words, but just as much when through his eager attention, through the assent or dissent expressed in his glances, he conjures words to the lips of the current speaker."[10] Rosenstock-Huessy's motto, *"Respondeo etsi mutabor!"* ("I respond *although* I will be changed!"), captures the element of risk to each partner that is involved when two people place them-

[8] Fritz Kaufmann, "Karl Jaspers and a Philosophy of Communication," in P. A. Schlipp (ed.) *The Philosophy of Karl Jaspers* (New York: Tudor, 1957), p. 214.

[9] *Ibid.* Cited from Eugen Rosenstock's "Introduction" to his correspondence with Franz Rosenzweig in the latter's *Briefe* (Berlin: Schocken Verlag, 1935), p. 638.

[10] Nahum N. Glatzer, *Franz Rosenzweig: His life and Thought* (New York: Schocken Books, Inc., 1953), p. 308.

selves under the spell of speech—that is, when a truly dialogical relationship develops.

Under such conditions dialogue differs very dramatically, it should be emphasized, from most of the so-called dialogues that one sees so often on educational and "public service" television programs. In such presentations the focus and the direction in which the exchange will proceed are almost always prearranged, the tone of the participants is to be "controlled," and "polite," and the program must begin and end within a specified time limit; even if there are no interruptions for commercial messages, such "dialogue" can be little more than a rather artificial and impersonal device for holding the attention of the unseen audience. In contrast, dialogue as exemplified in the Rosenstock/Rosenzweig correspondence is almost invariably in large measure unpremeditated, occurs without reference to any audience, and involves very serious risks for the participants.

Many of the references and allusions in the correspondence will seem familiar or unfamiliar to the reader according to the extent of his prior interest and involvement in the matters treated. Nevertheless, those who are interested, and surely those who are involved, in current discussion and debate on the role of Jew and Christian in our post-Christian era, and those who have a serious interest in the roles of speech, communication, and biblical hermeneutics in a secular age, will immediately recognize, or should, the profound relevance of this dialogue. But fascinating as this volume may be to students of the thought of Rosenstock-Huessy and Rosenzweig in particular, the real importance of the correspondence should rest primarily upon whether their method (i.e. that of "dialogue" and "speech-thinking"), and their insights into the relationship between Jew and Christian, are relevant to the passionate concerns of real people now and in the future. As Rosenzweig was to write later in another connection (specifically in regard to his and Martin Buber's plan to translate the Hebrew scriptures into German):

The time . . . is not ripe until a receptive people reaches out toward the wing beat of an alien masterpiece with its own yearning and its own utterance, and when its receptiveness is no longer based on curiosity, interest, desire for education, or even aesthetic pleasure, but has become an integral part of the people's historical development.[11]

The decision to make the biblical translation, a prodigious and ultimately fruitful undertaking, meant that in the period following World War I both Buber and Rosenzweig believed that the experience of an Eternal People, as recorded in the Old Testament was still meaningful for German-speaking peoples in the period following World War I. Similarly, the present validity of both the substance and the method of Rosenstock-Huessy's and Rosenzweig's dialogue depends in very large measure on whether or not the time is at last "ripe"—on whether there are now ears that wish, or are willing, to listen to what these men said to each other and to their age.

II

Little could Buber and Rosenzweig realize, as they began their pre-Hitler venture in biblical translation, the full and awful meaning for the Jews, and for all humanity, of the oft-cited words, "the stubbornness of the Jews"! Rosenzweig's unpremeditated preparation for that partnership with Buber began significantly in the now-famous conversation with Eugen Rosenstock in 1913, when the latter's "stubbornness" as a believing Christian, as a man who took revelation seriously, challenged the self-admitted relativism that was inherent in Rosenzweig's Hegelian philosophical bias. A non-practicing "Jew," Rosenzweig had studied history at Freiburg under Friedrich Meinecke in 1908–1912 and in July, 1913 he was still immersed in Hegel's political writings and German Idealism generally. Rosenstock, who had become a Christian at the age of sixteen, was a *Privatdozent* in the Faculty of Law at Leipzig, had published several books, and was generally a person whom the older Rosenzweig respected and admired. Later in life, in a letter to Meinecke dated August 30, 1920, Rosenzweig recalled the change that had come about in his life as a result of his encounter with Rosenstock and his (Rosenzweig's) subsequent

[11] *Ibid.*, p. 257.

conversion to Judaism. The letter was written to Meinecke from Frankfort, where Rosenzweig was conducting a "center for Jewish learning," the Freies Jüdisches Lehrhaus. "The man who wrote *The Star of Redemption*," Rosenzweig told Meinecke,

is of a different caliber from the author of *Hegel and the State*. Yet when all is said and done, the new book is only—a *book*. I don't attach any undue importance to it. The small—at times exceedingly small—thing called (by Goethe) "demand of the day" which is made upon me in my position at Frankfort, I mean the nervewracking, picayune, and at the same time very necessary struggles of people and conditions, have now become the real core of my existence—and I love this form of existence despite the inevitable annoyance that goes with it. Cognition [*Erkennen*] no longer appeals to me as an end in itself . . . . [whereas] the questions asked by human beings have become increasingly important to me. This is precisely what I meant by "cognition and knowledge as a service": a readiness to confront such questions, to answer them as best I can out of my limited knowledge and my even slighter ability. You will now be able to understand what keeps me away from the university . . .[12]

In another connection, Rosenzweig once said of Meinecke: "He treats history as though it were a Platonic dialogue, not murder and manslaughter."[13]

Rosenzweig's decisive rejection of Idealism, following his crucial encounter with Rosenstock in 1913, and his increasing preoccupation with the significance of revelation, was intensified in the course of his study of Schelling's writings and his discovery, in 1914, of a work by Schelling that had been attributed to Hegel. The influence of Schelling is quite evident in Rosenzweig's *The Star of Redemption* (1921), his opus magnum. But it is also readily apparent that Rosenstock's influence was equally powerful, if not more so. Only a very small part of a considerable body of evidence pointing in this direction can be alluded to here.

First, Rosenzweig's plan for the *Star* was inspired by his reading a "speech letter" from Rosenstock in 1916. This letter, written in

[12] *Ibid.*, pp. 96–97.
[13] *Ibid.*, p. 17.

response to Rosenzweig's request that his friend write to him on "the languages" (see Letter No. 21, p. 169 in the present volume), set forth the plan for, and much of the substance of, Rosenstock's *Angewandte Seelenkunde* (Applied Psychology, 1923), and prefigured (in outline form) the direction of Rosenstock's subsequent writings on sociology, speech, time, names, etc.—above all, his "cross of reality" as reflected in his "grammatical thinking."

Second, it was Rosenzweig's stated intention that the *Star* be read as a complement to *Angewandte Seelenkunde*. In the second part of the *Star*, for example, Rosenzweig applied the method of "speech-thinking," an approach to which he was introduced by Rosenstock and then adapted to his own purposes. The third part, devoted to the relationship between Jew and Christian, clearly reflects the decisive influence of his dialogue with Rosenstock on that subject.

Third, the significance of revelation, which first began to dawn on Rosenzweig as a result of his encouter with Rosenstock in 1913, and which was discussed at some length in the letters of 1916 (at Rosenzweig's request), serves as the cornerstone for Rosenzweig's resolution (in the second part of the *Star*) of the dilemma of philosophical Idealism as outlined in the first part. It is evident that Rosenzweig also drew heavily upon his reading of Schelling in 1914, but his discussion of revelation was influenced much more decisively by Rosenstock's insights.

Fourth, the influence of the later Schelling (in his *Philosophy of Revelation*, 1841) is evident in Rosenzweig's attack, in the first part of the *Star*, on the identity of Reason and Being in the philosophical systems of Kant and Hegel (as well as in *any* philosophy of religion that attempts to derive God's existence from a general notion of Being). Both Rosenzweig and Schelling embraced Idealism early in their lives but later rejected it in favor of a religious position that eventually was to be more orthodox than philosophical in character—and yet both, even after they had adopted a religious orientation, found it necessary to attempt a refutation of Idealism on the basis of a philosophical system. There are many parallels between Schelling's attack on the attempt by philosophical rationalists to identify experience with absolute reality, Mind with Spirit, in a rationally coherent system (in *Of Human Free-*

dom, 1795) and Rosenzweig's attack on Idealism in *The Star of Redemption*.

Fifth, in his essay on "The New Thinking" Rosenzweig stated, with respect to "influence," the following: "The main influence was Eugen Rosenstock; a full year and a half before I began to write I had seen the rough draft of his now published *Angewandte Seelenkunde*."[14]

III

As was suggested above, one principal merit of this present work, *Judaism Despite Christianity*, is that the past events dealt with—a dialogue of half a century ago—suggest a tone and climate for direction today. The dialogue bears significantly on a number of questions that are currently being raised and discussed, or, and perhaps more significantly, questions that *ought* be considered by those who are or will be concerned with the resonance of history and the works of the Spirit in years to come. Some of these problems—developments might be a better term—have to do with specifically religious concerns (ecumenicism, the "death of God" controversy, etc.); others are basically secular in nature.

First, consider for a moment the direction and impact of a number of contemporary trends among Jews and Christians. Following Pope John XXIII's declaration of January 25, 1959, the Twenty-First Ecumenical Council of the Roman Catholic Church was held, beginning on October 11, 1962, the first such council since Vatican I in 1869–1870. After it was over, Pope Paul VI, in reflecting upon nine centuries of religious division, spoke of *aggiornamento* and of the events of Vatican II as a plan and vision

[14] It should be noted that the "Letters on Judaism and Christianity" are but a relatively small part of the total correspondence between Rosenzweig and Rosenstock-Huessy and his wife, Margrit. Especially significant are the documents from the period when Rosenzweig was composing the first draft of *Der Stern der Erlösung*. Provisions have been made for the publication of some of this extremely important material at a later date. *Angewandte Seelenkunde* is reprinted in the first volume of Rosenstock-Huessy's *Die Sprache des Menschengeschlechts* (Heidelberg: Verlag Lambert Schneider, 1963), pp. 739–810. [See footnote 23 below.]

for subsequent ages to implement and realize. Among the official documents passed by the council was one concerning Christians and Jews and Christians and the adherents of other world religions (October, 1965). The document reads in part like an introduction to a course in comparative religion, but it does have the merit of giving considerable emphasis to the greatness of the "spiritual patrimony common to Christians and Jews," and to the desirability of fostering "mutual understanding and respect" and "brotherly dialogues" between them.[15]

This declaration is symptomatic of an ecumenical spirit that is playing an increasingly important role in contemporary religious activity, not only as between Jews and Roman Catholics but also in Protestant/Roman Catholic and Protestant/Jewish relationships. Rarely has Western man experienced such an ecumenically harmonious atmosphere. In the same breath it must be added, however, that to be meaningful and lasting "brotherly dialogues" must eventually touch the very marrow of fundamental spiritual *differences*. They must, for example, reach the point of recognizing mutual "stubbornness" on points of profound disunity—while at the same time continuing to exploit every possible opportunity for cooperative deliberation and action. This being so, the Rosenstock/Rosenzweig dialogue of 1916 continues to be of the greatest possible relevance. To some concerned readers, indeed, their letters may seem of far greater import, in the long run, than the document approved by the Council.

Even as "ecumenism" was becoming almost a household word in the 1960's, there suddenly burst upon the religious scene a number of pronouncements—most of them from sensitive Protestant clerics and theologians, but a few from Roman Catholic writers as well—to the effect that "God is dead!," and that the works of the Spirit can best be realized in a climate free from the parochialism of traditional religious institutional forms. A statement by the editor of *Prism*, cited by Bishop J. A. T. Robinson in his controversial best seller, *Honest To God*, captures the radical tone of these declarations:

[15] Walter M. Abbott, S. J., *The Documents of Vatican II* (New York: Guild Press, 1966), p. 665.

What certainly is true is that there are many men who find traditional religion and spirituality completely meaningless, and that you will find them among those who are completely committed to Christ as well as among those that are not . . . . We have reached a moment in history when these things are at last being said openly and when they are said there is an almost audible gasp of relief from those whose consciences have been wrongly burdened by the religious tradition.[16]

Thus, notwithstanding the strong emphasis on ecumenism in some religious circles, there is also much genuine concern about a growing shortage of ordinands for the ministry, and those responsible for theological education foresee the pressing necessity of a radical change in the very structure of the theological enterprise. In a recent matriculation address to the incoming class of a leading theological seminary in New York, for example, an eminent American church historian, Robert T. Handy, repeated the observations of a University of Cambridge don, Howard Root: " 'It is by no means clear that anything like Christian faith in the form we know it will ever again be able to come alive for people of our own time or of such future time as we can imagine,' " and then went on to say: ". . . we may be riveted by our past that we can hardly even imagine anything really new or different, either in the way Christian faith is stated or in the way it is institutionalized."[17]

And even among the more tradition-oriented supporters of ecumenism there are many who wonder whether the spirit that animated Vatican II can and will filter down and be felt at the local parish level. There are Roman Catholics who fear that reforms such as the introduction of the vernacular into the liturgy, hymn singing, and a better critical appreciation of the scriptural foundations of the faithful, may not be sufficient to enable the Church to participate effectively and creatively in what Harvey Cox has

[16] John A. T. Robinson, *Honest To God* (Philadelphia: Westminster Press, 1963), p. 141. See also Bishop Robinson's *Exploration into God* (Stanford: Stanford University Press, 1967).

[17] Robert T. Handy, *Do Not Let Your Minds Be Captured*. An address delivered at Union Theological Seminary, New York, on Sept. 25, 1963. Pp. 1–2.

described as the temporal/spiritual process of "secularization."[18] Bibliotry and poor imitations (at best) of many of the historic marks of traditional Protestant worship are regarded by some Catholics as questionable, if not inadequate, reforms, considering the fact that the value and relevance of those very same practices are being very seriously challenged by many Protestants themselves. If a certain traditional approach to worship no longer seems to "work" for Protestants, these Catholic critics wonder, is it likely that it will now be adequate for reform-minded Catholics?[19]

From a purely secular perspective, recent studies have shown, moreover, that despite the supposedly pervasive influence of the spirit of ecumenism, anti-Semitism is still a very serious "problem," not only among Roman Catholics but also—and even to a greater extent—among certain Protestant groups. There are also many indications that the Christian spirit of brotherly love, as applied in dealing with civil liberties and civil rights is a great deal more alive among Jews, Protestants, and Roman Catholics who are *less* "faithful" in their institutional observances (i.e. in attendance at formal religious services, etc.) than it is among Jews, Protestants, and Roman Catholics who are generally regarded—and who regard themselves—as "faithful" and "devout." Disparities of this kind account for—and perhaps justify, at least in part—a considerable amount of scepticism about the eventual consequences of the energy and the well-meaning publicity currently being invested in the ecumenical movement.[20]

[18] Harvey Cox, *The Secular City* (New York: The MacMillan Company 1965; rev. ed. 1966). Cox defines secularism as "any new closed world-view which functions very much like a new religion" (1965 ed., p. 21). Further: "While secularization finds its roots in the biblical faith itself," he continues, "and is to some extent an authentic outcome of the impact of biblical faith on Western history, this is not the case with secularism. Like any other ism, it menaces the openness and freedom secularization has produced . . . . Secularization arises in large measure from the formative influence of biblical faith on the world, an influence mediated first by the Christian Church and later by movements deriving partly from it."

[19] Cf. Daniel Callahan, "Post-Biblical Christianity," in *Commonweal*, LXXXV (Dec. 9, 1966) 10, pp. 291–93.

[20] Cf. C. Y. Glock & Rodney Stark, *Christian Beliefs and Anti-Semitism* (New York: Harper & Row, 1966); Selvin & Hagstrom, "Determinants

Thus it may well be that "ultimately," as Arthur Cohen has put it, "only individual Christians and individual Jews will form the new community of Church and Synagogue."[21] At a time when men everywhere are concerned with basically *human* problems, more often than not without any specific reference to the boundaries of confessionalism, there are serious representatives of every major religious tradition who are convinced that in an age such as ours the truly spiritual man must be one who is best described, in the words of Dietrich Bonhoeffer, as *homo non religious*. Hence Bonhoeffer's espousal of a "religionless Christianity" as, in his view, the only viable posture for speaking to a wide range of human needs that can no longer be dismissed as secular, profane, or purely human and thus not within the Spirit's province. Those within the traditional institutional religions who believe that such "profane" concerns are properly a part of the Spirit's domain, are understandably dismayed to find their own religious institutions seemingly incapable of coping with them.[22]

In addition to the widespread current interest in ecumenism and secularization in a "post-Christian" era there is a third area of interest to which this book is particularly relevant. I refer here to theological and (especially) secular interest in the theory and practice of "communication"—not only in religious and secular "dialogues" but in many areas of modern life, e.g. the revival of "tribalism" in various forms, and the effects and implications of

---

of Support for Civil Liberties," *British Journal of Sociology* (April, 1960), pp. 51–73; Alonzo & Kinch, "Educational Level and Support of Civil Liberties," *Pacific Sociological Review*, 7 (1964), p. 89–93. Moreover, there are many Catholics, including a large proportion of the laity who were presumably to benefit from Vatican II's reforms, who are finding the reforms not at all to their liking. Those of such mind seemingly prefer that their "religion" be largely separate from their daily lives—in many instances because the radical demands of Christianity are often in conflict with strongly held social, political, intellectual and/or racial prejudices.

[21] Arthur A. Cohen, "The Temper of Jewish Anti-Christianity," in David W. McKain, *Christianity: Some Non-Christian Appraisals* (New York: McGraw-Hill & Co., 1964), p. 209. Cf. in the same work, Franz Rosenzweig, "The Way Through Time: Christian History," pp. 191–203.

[22] Cf. Dietrich Bonhoeffer, *Letters and Papers from Prison* (New York: The Macmillan Company, 1962).

new developments in the electronic media. Both Rosenzweig and Rosenstock-Huessy, but most especially the latter, can now be seen to have been hermeneutical pioneers who anticipated, by many years, the work of Martin Heidegger, Rudolf Bultmann, Gerhard Ebeling, Ernst Fuchs, Martin Buber, Amos Wilder, *et al.* in recognizing and dealing with such matters as the philosophical and theological problems of demythologizing, problems of interpretation, speculation about the sacred potential of everyday human speech. Emphasis on the sacramental quality of language set within a Johannine framework was basic and central to Rosenstock-Huessy's thought, and, subsequently to Rosenzweig's, long before Karl Barth, Heidegger, and Bultmann made their principal contributions.[23]

The limitations of interpreting human language mainly from a theological perspective have been apparent to everyone involved

[23] The most readily available introductions at this writing are the Harper Torchbook edition (1966) of Rosenstock-Huessy's *The Christian Future, or the Modern Mind Outrun* (New York: Charles Scribner, 1946), and Nahum N. Glatzer's *Franz Rosenzweig: His Life and Thought* (New York: Schocken Books, 1953). Rosenstock-Huessy's interest in speech and language permeates all of his writings since before 1910. Cf. *Der Atem des Geistes* (Frankfurt am Main: Verlag der Frankfurter Hefte, 1951); *Heilkraft und Wahrheit: Konkordanz der politischen und der kosmischen Zeit* (Stuttgart: Evangelishes Verlagswerk, 1952); *Der unbezahlbare Mensch* (Berlin: Verlag Käthe Vogt, 1955); *Zurück in das Wagnis der Sprache* (Berlin: Verlag Käthe Vogt, 1957); *Soziologie* (Stuttgart: Kohlhammer, 2 vols., 1956 and 1958); *Das Geheimnis der Universitat* (Stuttgart: Kohlhammer, 1958); *Die Sprache des Menschengeschlechts* (Heidelberg: Verlag Lambert Schneider, 2 vols. 1963, 1964); and, most recently, the "autobiographical fragment," *Ja und Nein* (Heidelberg: Verlag Lambert Schneider, 1968). For a fuller listing of Rosenstock-Huessy's publications since 1910—more than 200 titles—cf. *Rosenstock-Huessy: Bibliography/ Biography* (New York: Four Wells, 1959). [N.B. All of the foregoing are available through Argo Books, Inc., Box 283, Norwich, Vt. 05055.] English translations of *Der unbezahlbare Mensch,* the *Soziologie* (2 vols.), *Die Sprache des Menschengeschlechtes* (2 vols.), and *Die Europäischen Revolutionen und der Charakter der Nationen* have been scheduled for publication by the University of Alabama Press in the next few years. See also Harold Stahmer, *"Speak that I May See Thee!": The Religious Significance of Language* (New York: The Macmillan Company, 1968), a study of the thought of J. G. Hamann, Eugen Rosenstock-Huessy, Franz Rosenzweig, Martin Buber, and Ferdinand Ebner.

in recent discussion of "radical religion" and "religionless Christianity." But with the exception of one of Rosenstock-Huessy's admirers, Harvey Cox, very few have discerned the close affinity that exists between the thought of Rosenstock-Huessy and that of communications experts like Buckminister Fuller and Marshall McLuhan. Many of the latter's more startling intuitions, important as they are, sound almost old hat—"familiar," certainly—to careful students of Rosenstock-Huessy's writings since World War I and before.

The ultimate impact of the electronic communications media on our present mechanical technological society is summed up in McLuhan's statement, "Today we appear to be poised between two ages—one of detribalization and one of retribalization." But we will soon find ourselves "playing the tape backward"—i.e. the tape that recorded human development from "tribal man to individual man."[24] In an increasingly "electronic age" we will move from a mechanical/technological way of life, geared to "individuals," to a "new" way in which "tribal" modes and values will be increasingly important. To those who are accustomed to separating reality into "subjects" and "objects," and who pride themselves on their ability to view things in "isolation" and "detachment"—that is, the vast majority of literate adults—the social and spiritual changes being brought about by the electronic revolution are bound to be rather disconcerting. It has been customary, for example, for students to regard with considerable scepticism, if not amusement, the suggestion that in the mythopoetic tribal mentality of the ancient Near East "inanimate objects" like trees and salt were viewed as *persons*, as *"thou's."* But now suddenly, with man on the threshold of a period dominated by electronic media, we hear communications specialists referring casually to man's "dialogue" with computing and programing machines.

"Cool terms" among those interested in communication in the arts and sciences are equally "cool" among those interested in the religious significance of human speech, in "speech-thinking," or in what some have called the "life of dialogue." Both groups, for example, assume that "style" (visual *vs.* oral, etc.) is and always

[24] Marshall McLuhan, *Understanding Media* (New York: McGraw Hill, 1965), p. 344.

has been a creative force in shaping, forming, the human environment; both groups are concerned with "relational" living, with the effect of external address—i.e. "the medium as the message"—upon our oral and aural powers; and lastly, both have delved into questions pertaining to the origin of language. Implicit in all this is a common renewed respect for the spoken word, which "involves all of the senses dramatically," and a concommitant and radical de-emphasis of man's merely visual perceptions and powers, which have played so dominant a role in the present technological period.[25]

IV

The late Dietrich Bonhoeffer will always remain an especially important figure for those interested in the thought of Franz Rosenzweig and, even more, that of Eugen Rosenstock-Huessy, owing to the depth of Bonhoeffer's commitment to historic religious orthodoxy and his insistence that contemporary man take seriously the fact that he must begin to speak and act as one living in a "post-Christian" era. Not only did he speak and act in terms of these convictions until his life was cut short by a Nazi hangman at Flossenbürg Prison on Monday, April 9, 1945, but his writings, perhaps more than those of any other single author, have helped to set the tone for much recent discussion of the quality of spirituality timely for our age.

Just as Bonhoeffer's writings seemed meaningful to only a handful of readers in Europe in 1945, so interest at that time in the writings of Rosenstock-Huessy and Rosenzweig was also extremely limited. The articles of Alexander Altmann and Dorothy Emmet concerning the Rosenzweig/Rosenstock-Huessy dialogue, first published in 1944 and 1945, and Rosenstock-Huessy's own *The Christian Future, Or the Modern Mind Outrun*, first published in 1946, did not reach—at least they were not appreciated by—a significantly large audience.[26]

[25] *Ibid.*, p. 77 ff. Cf. also the series of essays devoted to "The Electronic Revolution" in *The American Scholar*, 35 (Spring, 1966) 2.

[26] Cf. *The Journal of Religion*, XXIV (October, 1944) 4; XXV (October, 1945) 4.

But Bonhoeffer and Rosenstock-Huessy shared more than the fate of being understood only by relatively small groups of readers and listeners; far more importantly, the two men shared a number of common goals and interests. In an article entitled *Eugen Rosenstock-Huessy and Dietrich Bonhoeffer: Two Witnesses to the Change in our Time*, Bonhoeffer's sister, Mrs. Sabine Leibholz, writes: "Relating Eugen Rosenstock's teaching and activity and Dietrich Bonhoeffer's life and intellectual achievements does not require any artificial stimulation on my part, but in fact suggests itself. Both men believed, hoped, anticipated, and did much in common."[27] Their words have "come to life in many hearts," she writes, "but least of all in those of German theologians." Both men also knew the crucial importance of timing—that "everything has its time and every undertaking in the world has its hour." For each the essential insight is to "enter into the predicament of the whole, ready for sympathetic participation, and to draw self-sacrificingly from it ever new, unprecedented, and unknown thoughts and decisions."

As early as 1919 Rosenstock-Huessy had prophesied the impending "empire of lies" that would choke humanity under Hitler. In an essay published in that year, *Without Honor—Without Home*, he wrote: "Boundless anxiety will in the coming decades still drive many Germans to plans of revenge, attempts at restoration, and violent insurrections. We shall have to experience . . . an 'empire of lies,' because these forces will not rest until they are defeated. The Nationalist hates the Democrat, ... The Democrat hates the Nationalist, ..." The same ominous note was directed at the church as well: "The church has renewed the source of speech of the whole human race. Yet the word can dry up today . . . ." Rather than shrink from worldly contamination, Rosenstock declared, the church "must fall in love with the curses, because in them at least the first breath of a soul rises up. May the church listen! May the cry of the creature receive precedence. Only then can the church speak its second word."[28] At stake was the Word as human proclamation, as Bonhoeffer knew when he wrote: "The church must come out of its stagnation. We must

[27] Leibholz, p. 277.
[28] *Ibid.*, pp. 278–79.

risk saying controversial things. Our church, which in these years has fought only for its self-preservation, as if it were an end in itself, is incapable of being the bearer of the personal and redeeming word for mankind. For this reason earlier words must become powerless." Nevertheless, said Bonhoeffer, ". . . the day will come in which people will again be called upon to pronounce the word of God in such a way that the world will be changed by it. There will be a new language, perhaps quite unreligious, but as liberating and elevating as the language of Jesus. Until then, the concern of a Christian will be a quiet and hidden one. [And yet] there will be people who pray and do what is righteous and await God's time."[29]

Prior to 1933 few could have anticipated how "areligious" the Word would have to become in order to be effective. After 1933 it had to go underground in Germany, to manifest itself thereafter in the political language of resistance to Hitler. This was part of the price a man paid, the "cost of discipleship" as Bonhoeffer put it, of being an instrument of the Word. It was this kind of climate that led to the martyrdom of Bonhoeffer and others, and that led many of those who had been associated with Rosenstock-Huessy in his work camps of the 1920's—his "universities in the wilderness"—to join forces against Hitler in the famous Kreisau Circle. Those who had participated with Rosenstock in these camps regarded their works and their speech as being shaped by the Word. They were, in fact, prepared by experiences like this and others to see the language of political resistance to Hitlerism as but another form of sacred involvement. It is difficult for us today to appreciate the extremely limited and religiously conventional attitudes toward the Word that were held by a nation shaped by Lutheran theology and German Idealism. The work camps were one instance of a liberation from this tradition and made it possible for those associated with them to keep their ears attuned for the new speech patterns that the times would require of them. Of the Kreisau Circle, Bonhoeffer's sister wrote:

In the resistance to Hitler, Helmuth James Graf von Moltke, Peter Graf York von Wartenburg (Eugen Rosenstock's candidate for a doctor's degree), and others from this circle gave their lives. Rosen-

29 *Ibid.*, p. 279.

stock had in 1926 made the [educator] Adolf Reichwein, who in 1932 demonstratively went over to the Social Democratic Party of Germany (SPD), co-leader of the first labour camp. He was condemned to death in 1944. In 1928 Theodor Steltzer . . . tried to follow the example of the Silesian labour camp. He was always in contact with Hans Peters who [had] belonged to Rosenstock's faculty. Horst von Einsiedel, who [eventually] died in Sachsenhausen concentration camp, [had given] himself over completely to working with Eugen Rosenstock, who called him "The soul of the labour camps."[30]

As men of faith, both Bonhoeffer and Rosenstock-Huessy knew that the Word is active in the affairs of men only when there are creatures through whom the Word resounds. Whatever the catch phrase "death of God" means in different contexts, certainly those who resisted Hitler and tried to bring Europe and America to its senses during this human crisis knew that God could at least be "absent" wherever the Word was not alive on men's lips and burning in their hearts.

The implications of this shared sense of the meaning of the Word in terms of sacred human speech are apparent in both men's writings. Bonhoeffer developed this in a sketchy fashion in his discussions of the theme, "the world came of age" and in his religious anthropology. Rosenstock-Huessy has devoted most of his life in this century to "gnawing upon the bone of speech," especially since World War I and his pioneering *Sprachbrief* to Rosenzweig in 1916.[31] Problems of speech and language have been uppermost in his mind during this entire period and culminate in his *Die Sprache des Menschengeschlechts* (2 vols., 1963–1964). The same preoccupation permeates *Out of Revolution* (1938) and provides the heart of the plan for his two-volume *Soziologie* (1956–1958). The recent (1966) Harper Torchbook edition of *The Christian Future, or The Modern Mind Outrun* is undoubtedly the most readily accessible brief introduction to this aspect of Rosenstock-Huessy's writings and is an ideal complement to many of the themes developed in *Judaism Despite Christianity*.

[30] *Ibid.*, p. 281.
[31] Eugen Rosenstock-Huessy, *Die Sprache des Menschengeschlechts*, Vol. I, pp. 739–810.

Bonhoeffer's sister sees an intimate common commitment to imperative sacred speech in her brother's and Rosenstock-Huessy's writings. Visser t'Hooft said of Bonhoeffer, "Is not this hunger and thirst for reality, for being incarnated, for affirmative action and not only saying yes, the real key to Bonhoeffer's message?"[32] Mrs. Leibholz singles out this theme as the parallel key to Rosenstock-Huessy's life and cites as an illustration his remark (in *Die Sprache des Menschengeschlechts*): "In this way Christ produces again the real order between the spoken word and lived life. Words should be issued orders and proclaimed promises. Life should consist of executed orders and fulfilled promises. This is the real aim of all language since man first began to speak." Thus, she describes authentic "religiousness," in Rosenstock-Huessy's view, as "not a product of spiritual aptitudes, but rather it means that man is seized and called by God"—and as man answers, he thus "enters into mutuality and wins his reality."[33]

V

Thus far I have touched lightly on a number of themes, issues, and personalities that are seemingly disparate and unrelated but nevertheless fall into place within the context of the Jewish/Christian partnership that was developed by Rosenstock-Huessy and Rosenzweig after their first encounter in 1913.

An examination of Rosenzweig's major writings subsequent to 1913, most notably *The Star of Redemption* (1921) and his essay on *The New Thinking* (1925), reveals his continued preoccupation with Speech, Time, and Eternity as the keys to Jewish existence. In *Das neue Denken*, he acknowledged the primary and decisive formative influence of Rosenstock's *Angewandte Seelenkunde* on his own development of the method of "speech thinking" (*Sprachdenken*).[34] For each of them, the meaningfulness of language made sense, as Rosenstock wrote to Rosenzweig in 1916,

[32] Leibholz, p. 280.
[33] *Ibid*.
[34] Glatzer, p. 200.

"only for the people who had already suffered from philosophy before 1914." Positively, the partnership of Jew and Christian in language must be understood in terms of their conviction that mankind was on the threshold of a new age—the Johannine Age—and that *speech* would be the instrument for its realization and implementation. The Johannine millenarian theme was of course already quite well known to students of nineteenth-century Idealism, for it was a dominant motif in the writings of Fichte, Hegel, and Schelling. In Schelling's *Philosophy of Revelation*, for example, the millenarian idea of the successive "ages" of the world—the Petrine, Pauline, and finally the Johannine—is developed at length. These ages were linked by Schelling to three historic forms of Christianity: the Petrine age to Roman Catholicism, the Pauline age to Protestantism, and the Johannine age, i.e. the Age of the Spirit, to a new era marked by an absence of doctrinal and dogmatic concerns. "If I had to build a church in our time," Schelling declared, "I would dedicate it to Saint John."[35]

For Rosenstock-Huessy and Rosenzweig, the Johannine age would be an age ruled by the Word, and traditional barriers between the sacred and the profane would be eliminated. According to Rosenstock-Huessy, if the vision at the end of Revelation meant anything for John it served as a mark of "the New Jerusalem as a healing of the nations without any visible Church at its center." Early in *The Christian Future* he elaborates on John's vision by stating: "All things were made by the Word. In the beginning there was neither mind nor matter. In the beginning was the Word. St. John was properly the first Christian theologian because he was overwhelmed by the *spokenness* of all *meaningful* happening [emphasis supplied]."[36]

It is significant to view this Johannine orientation against a background of current discussion of a "post-Christian" era, or an era of "religionless Christianity," since "post-Christian" was precisely Dorothy Emmet's characterization, in 1945, of the spiritual climate wherein these exchanges occurred in 1913 and 1916. For

[35] Alexander Altmann, "Franz Rosenzweig on History," *Between East and West*, Altmann (Ed.) (London: East and West Library, 1958), p. 196.
[36] Rosenstock-Huessy, *The Christian Future*, pp. 129, 159–60.

both men, Johannine signified above all the possibility—in fact, the necessity—of replacing traditional institutional forms of spirituality with new speech forms and patterns. The age of the Spirit may need to be a totally *a*religious and *a*theological one. Rosenstock-Huessy suggests this when he says, in *The Christian Future*: "I believe that in the future, Church and Creed can be given a new lease on life only by services that are nameless and incognito." In another place he writes: "In the third epoch, beginning today, Christians must immigrate *into* our workaday world, there to incarnate the spirit in unpredictable forms." Why? Because ". . . *each generation has to act differently precisely in order to represent the same thing*. Only so can each become a full partner in the process of Making Man."[37] If this program does not exactly imply the "death" or "eclipse" of God, it suggests that new forms of spirituality must be discovered in order for the present "eclipse" to pass, or to put it another way, for a new "resurrection" of God in terms that can be accepted as meaningful and true for post-modern man.

VI

Rosenstock-Huessy's and Rosenzweig's characterization of the shape of spirituality in a "post-Christian" Johannine age is predicated on a rather unusual relationship between Jew and Christian, and it is at this juncture that post-Christian and ecumenical considerations are joined. The areligious quality of the age involves Jew and Christian in a partnership based on a mutual recognition of the validity of their respective claims, even though the claims of both are universal in scope and are therefore logically irreconcilable. The "stubbornness of the Jew" in the Christian's eyes is a necessary condition for their co-existence. Also implicit in the partnership is a rejection by both Jew and Christian of the notion that one is the "daughter" religion of the other, and of the notion that they share a common "Judaeo-Christian tradition." The success of the partnership *requires* that the Jew stub-

[37] *Ibid.*, pp. 127, 130.

bornly reject the Christian's claim that Jesus is the Messiah. Similarly, the Christian no longer needs the Jew's *Old* Testament, since the traditions of the church have indeed become the Christian's historical past—his own testimony to the belief that Jesus is the Christ. The Jew rests all claims for his uniqueness upon his "stubborn" insistence that the Jews have known from the beginning that "God is One." Because of his audacity and his refusal to accept the Christian claim that Jesus is the Messiah, the Jew remains historically rejected and despised.

However, the Jew *already* lives in the *eschaton* (the end), the goal towards which the Christian strives to direct all history. The Jew already lives *from* and *in* Eternity—he already stands at the very end of history—and thus he constitutes a living testimony, for those (i.e. Christians) who struggle within an historical, eschatological framework, to the fact that history does have a goal. Thus the role of the Jew is an ahistorical one, whereas the Christian lives constantly *in* the world (in history) as a mediator to the Gentile of that saving Eternal knowledge which the Jew has carried in his heart, and from which he has suffered since the beginning of time. That history and mankind have not yet been redeemed needs no apology, so far as the Christian is concerned, for only when that End Time has come will the perverseness of the Jew be understood in retrospect by men everywhere as a sign of their own perversity and incompleteness. Were the Jew not to exist in his own terms *despite* the claims of Christianity, then the source of the claim of the Christian to be "in" and yet not "of" the world would be forgotten, and the Christian would soon lose his distinctive identity; he would relapse into paganism and thus be merely of the world. The "stubbornness of the Jew," then, is a constant reminder to the Christian not only that there is purpose and meaning in history but also that history as such is not that purpose and so can not of itself provide an adequate *raison d'être*. Though the Johannine Age will be "areligious" and "post-Christian," new speech patterns can only be redemptive—historically meaningful—if there remains until the "end of time" both an ahistorical reference and persons who are committed to the redemption of Time and History.

In sum, without the Word, Eternity will not become a universal fact; without the Presence of Eternity, the Word will not become the master and instrument but will be merely the servant and pawn of "purposeless" historical relativism.

VII

In the perspective of human experience, the context in which our words are spoken, our deeds done, is history. Thus, the original encounter between Eugen Rosenstock and Franz Rosenzweig in 1913 occurred within a historical context and involved an encounter between the believer, Rosenstock, and the then agnostic, historical relativist, Rosenzweig. From a historical, human experiential perspective, human speech as the Word Incarnate—as, in Rosenstock-Huessy's phrase, "the fruit of our lips"—constitutes the primary bulwark against all forms of agnosticism and unbelief. Paradoxically, the significance of the "emancipation of Jewry" often requires—so it seems—the presence of the Christian slave of the Word to remind both the "emancipated Jew" and the "secularized Christian" that history and the "secular" do not, and indeed cannot, provide their own rationale. Within this setting, revelation as the Word Incarnate, shapes and is shaped by history. For J. G. Hamann, and for all those who have accepted the sacramental qualities inherent in the fraility and tentativeness of human speech, the ambiguities and relativity of history could not possibly be denied. Both Rosenstock-Huessy and Rosenzweig certainly knew full well that what one holds to be "objectively" true, at the moment, is conditioned by time and history, and that perfect objectivity is simply not possible; in dealing with ultimate ontological questions, man is seemingly doomed to perpetual embarrassment and frustration.

In considering Rosenstock-Huessy and Rosenzweig it is appropriate, then, to speak of their "objective relativism." For this term conveys a sense of their awareness of the fragility and uncertainty of the human condition while maximizing the enduring durability of words uttered at the "right time"—the "proper season." Words uttered under such pressures are not validated by specific "blood ties," since the option is a historical one for all men. If the Cross symbolizes the Christian mission in historic space and time, and if the Jew lives ahistorically from Eternity to Eternity, then it is the Spirit (in the Johannine sense) that inspires our words when we have occasion to speak out of a sense of historical necessity. However, the sense of urgency and the hope of realization are made available to such frail mortals who speak for just so long as the "stubbornness of the Jew" remains a historical fact *despite* Christianity. From such a perspective, for the believing Jew and Christian the future remains, in fact and in truth, a spoken Epilogue to Eternity.

Harold Stahmer

Barnard College
January, 1968

1

ABOUT THE CORRESPONDENCE:

Essays by Alexander Altmann
and Dorothy M. Emmet

Franz Rosenzweig and Eugen Rosenstock-Huessy:
An Introduction to Their "Letters on Judaism & Christianity"
by Alexander Altmann*

The "Letters on Judaism and Christianity" of Franz Rosenzweig and Eugen Rosenstock have rightly been described as
one of the most important religious documents of our age.[1] The
two correspondents face each other not as official spokesmen of
their respective faiths but as two human beings who are aware
both of their separateness as Jew and Christian and their oneness
in Adam. They meet, as Rosenstock once put it,[2] "under the
open sky." They express but their own views; and it is precisely
this informal, personal, and direct character in their meeting
which brings out a depth of thought and a frankness of expression
that is unparalleled in the long history of Jewish-Christian re-

* Dr. Alexander Altmann is Philip W. Lown Professor of Jewish Philosophy at Brandeis University. His essay is reprinted, with minor editorial
revisions, from *The Journal of Religion* (October, 1944), with the kind
permission of the University of Chicago Press and Dr. Altmann.

[1] Cf. H. J. Schoeps, *Jüdisch–Christliches Religionsgespräch in 19 Jahr-
hunderten* (Berlin, 1937), p. 120.

[2] In a letter to Miss Dorothy M. Emmet.

lations. Unlike the medieval disputations, in which dogma was arrayed against dogma and verse set against verse, this discussion is a true dialogue. It is indeed the most perfect example of a human approach to the Jewish-Christian problem. It is also an exemplification of what is called the "existential" attitude to theological problems, in that it breaks down the artificial barrier between *theologumena* and *philosophumena* and considers its subject from an all-round human viewpoint, instead of isolating it.

The present analysis is concerned with the history and background of this important correspondence. It does not enter into an elucidation of the correspondence itself, which is a task that may be reserved for a later opportunity. Everybody who has read these letters will agree that they require an introduction. It is hoped that the present article may serve this purpose and, at the same time, encourage those who are as yet unacquainted with the letters to read and study them.

Franz Rosenzweig and Eugen Rosenstock met for the first time at Leipzig University in 1913. Rosenstock was lecturer in medieval constitutional law, and Rosenzweig, though two years older, was his pupil. He had studied medicine, turned to history and philosophy, written a thesis on *Hegel und der Staat*, and now felt the importance of some training in law. As early as 1911, theology had been added to the subjects to which he was devoting himself "in an unbounded receptivity."

When he met Rosenstock, he found in him not only a jurist and historian but a philosopher as well.[3] Both of them were aware of the discrepancy that existed between the great philosophical heritage of 1800 and the sterility of philosophy in their own generation. Nietzsche had put forward the just claims of the human element in any philosophical approach to the world and history. He had asked for a type of philosopher who was not only a great thinker but a complete human being. The generation of 1910 began to understand how legitimate this claim was. In the years just before and during the Great War, a fundamentally new philosophical approach was gathering strength. The "existential" philosopher was emerging from the barrenness of the

[3] See Letter No. 2.

27

schools. The importance of the "existential" factors of personal decision and response was being recognized in determining that generation's philosophy. This soon became clear in theology, to which new depth was being given by Karl Barth. In philosophy, a new irrationalism (Stefan George and his group; Georg Simmel in Germany, Henri Bergson in France) at first obscured the rise of the new "existential" philosophy, but the movement was gaining more and more ground. It expressed itself most notably in the new branches of phenomenology, which sprang from Edmund Husserl's renewal of scholasticism; in Max Scheler's philosophy of values; and, finally, in Martin Heidegger's ontology.

There is evidence that, in some measure, Rosenzweig had worked his way through to an "existential" philosophy even before he met Rosenstock, though the decisive turn toward the "new thinking"[4] was undoubtedly due to Rosenstock's influence. In 1909 Rosenzweig and a circle of friends had met with the purpose of forming a society to save the ripe achievements of the nineteenth century (social progress, the historical approach, nationalism, the scientific attitude) in the twentieth century, so as to possess them no longer as mere objects of a struggle but as elements of a new civilization.[5] The scheme failed; but what Rosenzweig had felt to be the cardinal point of his and his friends' endeavors, namely, that they wanted to realize 1900 as distinctively different from 1800, still remained his guiding star. In a letter to Hans Ehrenberg (September 26, 1910),[6] Rosenzweig emphasized how the twentieth century had departed from the Hegelian view of history. To us, he says, history is no longer something to be contemplated but something to be acted upon. This has, he feels, a vital bearing on theology. Hegel's religious "intellectualism" is no longer ours. Today we emphasize the practical moment, sin, actual history. History can no longer be interpreted as a divine process developed in time and to be contemplated by the onlooker but has to be recognized as the sum

[4] Cf. Rosenzweig's essay, "Das neue Denken," *Kleinere Schriften* (Berlin, 1937), p. 373.

[5] Franz Rosenzweig, *Briefe* (Berlin: Schocken Verlag, 1935), p. 49.

[6] *Briefe*, pp. 50, 53.

total of human actions. It does not present an impersonal process but personal actions, relations, and meetings. Therefore, we refuse to see "God in history" because we do not want to look on history as a picture or as a being that unfolds. We recognize God in every human being of ethical value, but not in the accomplished whole of history; for why should we be in need of a God, if history were godlike, if every deed, once it entered history, became *ipso facto* godlike and justifiable? No, he says, every human deed is liable to become sinful precisely after it has entered history and has become part of it, since through the interrelation of acts in history no act is merely personal but is caught up in an impersonal nexus of cause and effect beyond the control and intention of the doer. For this reason God must redeem man, not through history, but—there is no alternative—through religion. For Hegel and his "school" history was divine theodicy; for us religion is the only true theodicy. Thus Rosenzweig felt that the twentieth century's attack on the nineteenth century's interpretation of history paved the way for a new and deeper understanding of religion.

This new approach to religion had, however, to wait for its actual embodiment in his life and work until he met Rosenstock about three years later. The union of philosophy and theology that was to become the main feature of the "new thinking" could be brought about only by an experience of the reality of religion, not by mere academic reflections. Though some of the sentences quoted could have been written by Kierkegaard, Rosenzweig was still far from a standpoint of faith. The reason must be sought in Rosenzweig's personal situation as a Jew without actual roots in Jewish tradition. He was the son of an old Jewish family that had lost most of its Jewish heritage. True, there was a certain loyalty to the old faith and community, both on his and on his parents' part.[7] But it was of no vital importance to him. And, rather than pretend to be a Jew, he tried to ignore the fact, seeing that, assimilated as he was to German cultural life, his mind had already become Christianized. "We are Christians in every respect," he once expressed himself in an outburst of sincerity; "we live in a Christian state, attend Christian schools, read

[7] Cf. *ibid.*, pp. 25, 31.

Christian books, in short, our whole civilization is fundamentally Christian," he wrote in a letter to his parents (November 6, 1909). There was nothing, he felt, that divided him from his Christian friends.[8] But he failed to see that there was a breach within his own being and that he was unable to find his inner form of life until that breach was closed.

The discussions he had with Rosenstock during the summer of 1913 led to a crisis in his life. Not only did Rosenstock share with Rosenzweig a sense of dissatisfaction with contemporary philosophy and a strong tendency toward "existential" philosophy; he seemed actually to personify the new type of philosopher that Rosenzweig was striving so hard, and yet in vain, to become. Rosenstock not only taught but lived his philosophy. The experience of his oneness could not fail to impress Rosenzweig. He was faced with a thinker who was living in accordance with his faith, and this faith was not a naïve return to the old dogma but a reinterpretation of the old faith in a new philosophical language. The "philosophy of speech," which was later to play so great a part in Rosenzweig's own thinking, had already been conceived by Rosenstock, it seems, at the time the two met in Leipzig. According to it, truth is revealed through speech as expressing the intercommunication of one mind with another. It is not the formal truths of logic in their timeless, abstract, systematic character that are really vital and relevant, but rather the truths that are brought out in the relationships of human beings with God and with one another—truths that spring from the presentness of time and yet reach out into the eternal. The I—Thou relationship is the central theme of this philosophy of speech, as against the I—It relationship of traditional philosophy. The truths of revelation are identical with the truths of the I—Thou relationship. The "word" (in the biblical sense) is superior to the logos of philosophy. The "word" springs from meeting and response. It has the character of a dialogue, whereas the logos has the nature of a monologue. Rosenzweig was to formulate these ideas and their deeper implications later in his magnum opus— *The Star of Redemption*[9]—and more concisely in his essay on

[8] Cf. *ibid.*, p. 72.
[9] *Der Stern der Erlösung* (Frankfurt, 1921).

"The New Thinking" (1925). To what extent his philosophy of speech was developed in 1913 is difficult to establish. But its basic character, i.e., the existential attitude, was certainly there.

The discussions between the two reached their climax in a memorable night's conversation on July 7, 1913, which is frequently referred to in the correspondence and forms its permanent background. It was the most decisive and most far-reaching event in Rosenzweig's inner life. It produced a crisis from which, after months of struggle, the new Rosenzweig eventually emerged.

If one puts together the various references to that night's conversation both in the correspondence and in an important letter to Rudolf Ehrenberg, one is able to form a fairly clear picture of how it developed. Rosenstock himself gives a brief account of it in his Preface to the publication of the correspondence.[10]

[10] *Briefe*, pp. 638–39: As translated by Miss Dorothy Emmet:

"This exchange of letters, dating from the third year of the World War, is concerned with the perennial, essential, supra-personal questions of the life of the Jew and the Christian among the peoples of the world, with their 'theological existence today' ['*Theologische Existenz heute*,' the series title of pamphlets issued by Karl Barth]. Thanks to the abnormal tension in people's minds, which isolated them from the rest of the world at that time, the letters are entirely free from any consideration as to whether they would do good or harm. The 'Jewish question' and the 'Christian question' appear here in a purely introspective form, in a way that is not normally possible because of the nature of the subject.

"Even the two correspondents themselves were only forced to an uncompromising display of their positions after hesitation and to their own surprise. But for that reason the subjective and personal element in the letters should not irritate the reader. Moreover, this element provides the indispensable supply of fuel without which the most matter-of-fact dialogue cannot be kindled. Nor ought the passionate character of the discussion detract at all from its objective truth. The letters themselves mention at some length the thought that only in the extreme necessity of spiritual self-defense is there a chance of learning the truth about the questions that touch one's own life. And Franz Rosenweig again dealt with this method of thinking several times before his death.

"The two correspondents get into their stride only haltingly. This is explained also by the fact that there was a gap of nearly three years in their exchange of ideas. This was broken after a conversation, which still leaves its echoes in the letters between three people in the summer of 1913, a summer which both correspondents had spent in Leipzig, the

In 1913 Rosenzweig and Rosenstock had opposed each other, not as a Jew and as a Christian, but as "faith in philosophy" against "faith based on revelation." The Christian was confronted with a Jew whose sense of Judaism was not strong enough to face him. He considered his friend's Judaism merely as "a kind of personal idiosyncrasy, or at best as a pious romantic relic of the posthumous influence of a dead great uncle"—a reference to Rosenzweig's great-uncle, Adam Rosenzweig, who had some considerable influence on his nephew—and he felt justified in putting it "in inverted commas."[11] Rosenzweig was forced "to lay bare his own skeleton and to examine his own anatomy."[12] His opponent compelled him to take a stand, and eventually defeated him. Rosenzweig wrote some three months later:

In that night's conversation Rosenstock pushed me step by step out of the last relativist positions that I still occupied, and forced me to take an absolute standpoint. I was inferior to him from the outset, since I had to recognize for my part too the justice of his attack. If I could then have buttressed my dualism between revelation and the world with a metaphysical dualism between God and the Devil [he meant to say if he could have split himself into two halves, a religious and a worldly one], I should have been unassailable. But I was prevented from doing so by the first sentence of the Bible. This

one as *Privatdozent*, the other in private study. This conversation too was concerned with questions of faith. But it was not Judaism and Christianity that were then arrayed against each other, but rather faith based on revelation was contrasted with faith in philosophy. From this difference of orientation in that last important conversation, the difficulties in understanding which make themselves felt in the letters are explicable. It was just these difficulties which served to call forth a growing measure of clarity.

"A word must be said about the external occasion which set the correspondence going, because it plays a part at the beginning of the letters. The third participant in the religious discussion of the summer of 1913, Rudolf Ehrenberg, visited Eugen Rosenstock in Kassel, and the latter further utilized his short stay on military business in his friend's home town in order to obtain publication of 'The Original Program of German Idealism,' which Rosenzweig had discovered in Berlin before the War. It was in fact accepted during the War by the Heidelberg Academy of Sciences in its record of Proceedings."

[11] See Letter No. 9.
[12] See Letter No. 9.

piece of common ground forced me to face him. This has remained even afterwards, in the weeks that followed, the fixed point of departure. Any form of philosophical relativism is now impossible to me.[13]

The change in Rosenzweig's philosophical outlook can be clearly seen in two letters to Hans Ehrenberg, written in December of the same year.[14] They concern the relationship between faith and reason, revelation and philosophy. What happens in history, he says, is not a struggle between man's faith and man's reason but a struggle between God and man. In world history the absolute powers themselves are *dramatis personae*. Revelation breaks into the world and transforms creation, which is the Alpha of history, into redemption, which is the Omega. Philosophy has a pagan quality. It is an expression of the Alpha, of creation, of pure nature to which God has given freedom—even against himself. But as revelation comes into the world, it gradually absorbs philosophy, deprives it of its pagan elements, and illuminates it with its own light. The Omega of history will be realized after the element of creation, the world's freedom, has spent itself. Then God, who has allowed the world to be the Alpha, will again be the First and the Last, the Alpha and the Omega.

Rosenzweig believed (cf. the two letters mentioned just above) that the absorption of philosophy into the realm of revelation was not merely a postulate of faith but a historical fact. Medieval scholasticism meant the adoption and transformation of Greek, i.e., pagan, philosophy. The reformations of the sixteenth century could not alter the fact that the spiritual world of Europe had already been Christianized; on the contrary, they only confirmed it. Though faith and reason had again been separated, Descartes, Spinoza, and Leibniz were no longer pagans, but they were Christian heretics; and their spiritual descendants, e.g., Kant, Fichte, Schelling, and Hegel, actually returned into the fold of Christianity. Rosenzweig felt that, whatever pagan tendencies may have been left alive in philosophy, they could not have any decisive influence in the post-Hegelian world, because in Hegel's

[13] *Briefe*, p. 71.
[14] Cf. *ibid.*, p. 79.

33

philosophical idealism the Greek, i.e., pagan, spirit had spoken its last word. Hegel marked the *finis philosophiae*. "From Thales to Hegel" or "from Ionia to Jena," as Rosenzweig put it in *The Star of Redemption*, the history of philosophy was identical with the history of philosophical idealism. It was the declared aim of every philosopher to reduce "everything" (God, world, man) to a single principle—to identify *every*thing with *one* thing. It tried to reduce God and man to the cosmos (in ancient philosophy), man and the world to God (in medieval philosophy), or God and the world to man (in modern philosophy).[15] In Hegel this tendency overreached itself, insofar as he attempted not only to derive everything from the absolute mind but also to comprehend the historical process of philosophical thought as a process of logical necessity. Thus, in Hegel's system the problems of idealistic, i.e., pagan, philosophy are finally settled. No further step beyond is possible. After Hegel there can be no more philosophers in the idealistic, i.e., pagan, fashion but only philosophers of faith, Christian philosophers. The monologues of the idealistic philosophers have now to be replaced by the dialogues of human beings with faith and common sense.[16] Instead of identifying everything with everything, man has to recognize the distinctiveness and separateness of the three entities which are God, man, and the world; but at the same time he has to realize the interrelations that exist between them. Those who in the post-Hegelian period are still trying to philosophize after the old pagan fashion are condemned to sterility. The barrenness of the "schools," about which Rosenzweig had complained before, now seemed to him quite understandable, though not pardonable. The so-called philosophers of the post-Hegelian period he could no longer regard as "philosophers" but merely as professors, doctors. Hegel was the last "philosopher."

But Hegel was not only the last philosopher. He was also "the first of the new Church Fathers," as Rosenzweig would call him.[17] The world *post-Hegel mortuum* had entered upon a period of spiritualized Christianity. The absorption of pagan philosophy

15 Cf. *Kleinere Schriften*, pp. 377 ff.
16 See Letter No. 17.
17 Cf. *Briefe*, p. 81.

by the church had been completed by 1800. "Since 1800 the Greeks are no longer a power (and no longer a burden)."[18] Rosenzweig would later call the new age "the Johannine period" of Christianity, a term he borrowed from Schelling. Schelling had said that if he was to build a new church he would consecrate it to John, because he preached the gospel of the logos.[19] In the past, the Church Fathers had had to work out the dogma, the "word of self-consciousness." Now the task was a different one. The task was not so much to elaborate what the church wanted to know for itself, i.e., the dogma, but to address itself to the Gentiles. We should interpret Rosenzweig correctly by saying that the task, in his opinion, was not to continue the monologue of dogmatic thought (which was bound up with the need for absorbing pagan philosophy) but to start the dialogue of speech, of personal approach, now that the pagan element was already absorbed. There could no longer be any serious conflict between philosophy and faith, since philosophy had found its place within the church.

It appears that Rosenzweig adopted this new philosophy of faith immediately after that night's conversation with Rosenstock. It solved for him the problem of philosophy and faith and enabled Rosenzweig to combine his favorite idea of the contrast between 1800 and 1900 with a new and comprehensive outlook on the history of philosophy and revelation. Rosenzweig the historian and philosopher was merged into Rosenzweig the religious thinker. But his new theory, though it settled the conflict between philosophy and faith, seriously embarrassed his position as a Jew. If it was the function of Christianity to convert the heathen and to transform the Alpha element of creation —the world in its raw state—into the Omega element of redemption—the world as the place of revelation—was there any room left for Judaism? Was not the life of Israel throughout the ages one of seclusion, expressing itself primarily in the law, instead of seeking contact with the pagan world of philosophy? Was not even Jewish scholasticism in the Middle Ages and Jewish philosophy in modern times an expression only of the periphery of

[18] *Ibid.*, p. 82.
[19] Cf. *Kleinere Schriften*, p. 266; *Briefe*, p. 91.

35

Jewish life, not of its inner concern? How could revelation in this completely inward form hope to conquer the world? At a later stage Rosenzweig was to recognize the vital importance of the Jewish form of religious life, not only for Israel, but for the church itself. But it seems that at first sight the aloofness and separation of the Jewish people from the world indicated to him a hopeless sterility and a lack of meaning and purpose in its continued existence. He felt that the medieval figures of the church and the synagogue were right in representing the one as holding a scepter and the other with a broken staff and bandages before her eyes. The symbolism of these figures runs through Rosenzweig's letters. The year 313 (Constantine) had opened for Christianity "the road through the world," the highway of the church militant. That road was the opposite of the one that the year 70 had opened to the Jew. Previously, Rosenzweig had agreed with Eduard Schwartz's theory—which represented the Protestant view—that the year 313 meant "the beginning of a falling away from true Christianity." But now he reversed his opinion. He would no longer begrudge the church its scepter because he saw that the synagogue was holding a broken staff. He would no longer "Judaize" his view of Christianity. And the question forced itself upon him as to whether there was any purpose in the further existence of the synagogue, seeing that in the reality of history the struggle between the pagan world and the message of revelation was being fought out not by Judaism, but by Christianity.[20]

What was Rosenzweig's answer to this disturbing question? His first reaction was an impulse to leave the synagogue and to become a member of the church. "In this world—since I did not, and still do not, recognize anything outside the world unrelated to what is inside—in this world, then, there did not seem to be any place for Judaism."[21] He was determined to carry his conviction to its final conclusion. He decided to become a Christian. But this resolution was never carried out. In the three months between July and October, 1913, he struggled desperately to find his place. He made a reservation. Before becoming a Chris-

[20] *Briefe*, p. 72.
[21] *Ibid.*

tian he wanted to live as a Jew. He felt that he should not enter the church through the intermediary stage of paganism, but as a Jew. This reservation helped him to establish a new and more serious relationship with the world of Judaism, which hitherto he had considered only from the standpoint of the Christian philosopher. Now the deadly earnestness of his crisis forced him to face Judaism as a Jew, and the result was that Judaism conquered him. He wrote to his mother, on October 23: "You will have learned from this letter that I have found the way back which, for almost three months, I had struggled for in vain."[22] And to Rudolf Ehrenberg he wrote a few days later, on October 31:

Dear Rudi:

I have something to tell you which will disturb you, at least for the moment, and which will be incomprehensible to you. After long, and I believe searching, consideration, I have arrived at the point of taking back my resolution. It seems to me no longer necessary and, therefore, in my case, no longer possible. So I am remaining a Jew.[23]

It would be wrong to assume that Rosenzweig's decision to remain a Jew involved a change in the philosophy to which Rosenstock had converted him. The two letters to Hans Ehrenberg, from which we quoted above in outlining his new philosophy of faith, were written in December, 1913, *after* he had decided to remain a Jew. The interesting feature about Rosen-

[22] *Ibid.*, pp. 65–70.

[23] *Ibid.*, p. 71. [When writing this essay in 1944, the author was unaware of the important fact disclosed by Rosenzweig's disciple and friend Nahum N. Glatzer in 1952 that Rosenzweig's decision to remain a Jew was ultimately the result of a religious experience and happened with the force of a conversion. The letters to his mother and to R. Ehrenberg were written immediately after he had attended the service of the Day of Atonement, 1913. He "left the service a changed person. What he had thought he could find in the church only—faith that gives one an orientation in the world— he found on that day in a synagogue." See Nahum N. Glatzer, "Franz Rosenzweig: The Story of a Conversion," *Judaism: A Quarterly Journal of Jewish Life and Thought*, Vol. I, No. 1 (January 1952) pp. 70–71. Cf. also Glatzer's book *Franz Rosenzweig, His Life and Thought* (Second, Revised Edition, New York, 1961), p. 25. In the light of this biographical fact Rosenzweig's previous struggles assume the character of a *preparatio Judaica*.]

zweig's final position, which he reached in October, is the new insight into the compatibility of Judaism and Christianity "within the same realm." What he had worked out for himself with regard to the function of the church militant in the history of the world remained true and valid. But, whereas he had previously failed to see any purpose in the life of the synagogue, because of her broken staff and the bandages before her eyes, he now perceived the meaning of the synagogue as well. He recognized that her stern refutation of the pagan world and her uncompromising attitude constituted the only safeguard for the completion of the work of revelation and of the church herself. The church, taking her road through the world, was always in danger of compromising with the world and its pagan instincts. The conquered might give her their laws. Christianity might be interpreted in the sense of a pagan philosophy. It might become identified either with a myth or with a philosophical system. But the existence of the people of Israel served as a reminder that revelation comes from God not from the natural mind, from the Jews not from the Greeks. In Israel's seclusion from the world, in its priestly way of life, it expresses the essence of revelation in an absolute form, unalloyed by any element of paganism. The synagogue, whose life is ruled by the law, not by a philosophy and not even by a dogma, may be lacking in the power of articulate speech. The synagogue may be unable to convey the contents of revelation to the pagan world. But her very existence is inarticulate speech. She is the "mute admonisher," who reminds the church, whenever she might become entangled in the life of this world, its nations and its empires: "Master, remember the last things." For this reason synagogue and church, though they are exclusive, are actually complementary and call for each other.[24]

Rosenzweig had discovered his identity with the Jewish doctrine. He wrote to Rudolf Ehrenberg:

[24] Cf. *ibid.*, p. 73. [See now the author's essay "Franz Rosenzweig on History," in *Between East and West: Essays Dedicated to the Memory of Bela Horovitz*, ed. by Alexander Altmann (London, 1958), pp. 194–214; reprinted in the author's *Studies in Religious Philosophy and Mysticism* (London and Ithaca, N.Y., 1969).]

You will have noticed already that in my theory I am no longer borrowing from Christianity. . . . I feel myself now in the most important points . . . above all in my deviation, insofar as I have expressed it, namely, in the doctrine of sin, in perfect and unintentional agreement with the Jewish doctrine, whose evidence in Jewish cult and life I had disputed before, but now recognize. As I said before, I am about to interpret to myself the whole system of Jewish doctrine on its own Jewish basis.[25]

Like the explorer of a new continent, he threw himself into the world of Judaism. A fresh vitality took possession of him. But he himself knew too well that he stood only at the beginning. He had found his way back to Judaism, but he was still far from being a Jew in the same sense as Rosenstock was a Christian. He was not yet strong enough to face his opponent again. But he knew the day would come when they would meet once more and that the second meeting would no longer be one between a Christian and a philosopher, but one between a Christian and a Jew. For this meeting he had to prepare himself.

In November, 1913, a month after he had found his way back to Judaism, he made the acquaintance of Hermann Cohen, the great neo-Kantian, who, in his retirement from the professorial chair in Marburg, was lecturing in Berlin. Moved by a certain curiosity, Rosenzweig went to one of his lectures. He held no brief, as we know, for post-Hegelian philosophers and did not expect anything. But he found more than a celebrated professor. He found "a philosopher and a man," a "great soul," a "religious person."[26] He became Cohen's disciple and intimate friend. There are some references to Rosenzweig's reverence for Cohen in the correspondence. They betray a certain reluctance to reveal his true feelings for Cohen. But from other sources we are able to draw a fuller picture of the impression Cohen made on him and the influence he had on his future development.

When Rosenzweig met the old philosopher, a life of fame lay behind Cohen, who was the recognized head and master of a school, the author of a system of philosophy that claimed to comprehend the whole range of human culture. He was a "new

[25] *Briefe*, pp. 75–76.
[26] *Kleinere Schriften,* pp. 291 ff.

Hegel," as Rosenzweig called him,[27] in the sense that he represented the history of philosophy—which to Cohen was identical with the history of "critical idealism"—as a logical process, as the history of human reason. In a trilogy of books, like Kant in his three Critiques, Cohen had built up a system of his own. He wanted to crown it with a "psychology of civilization," which was to include the achievements of the nineteenth century. But the "Hegelianism of this neo-Kantian" was not carried to its conclusion. The religious element in Cohen revolted. Throughout his life he had struggled to find religion a place somewhere in the system of culture. Now he began to realize that he had to sacrifice the basic principle of idealism, the absolute sovereignty of the mind, in order to do justice to religion. In his lectures during the winter term of 1913–14 and in the summer of 1914, he introduced a new category of thought, which he called "correlation" and which expressed, fundamentally, much the same idea as the I—Thou philosophy that Rosenstock and Rosenzweig had evolved. [*N.B.*: See the *"Editor's Note"* following Miss Emmet's essay, p. 69.] With this new conception he broke down the "magic circle" of idealism in which God and man had been caught as mere functions in a system. Now he perceived them in their separateness and individuality, in their personal existence and their relations to each other. The "pagan" philosopher Cohen had become a theologian or, rather, a philosopher of faith. Rosenzweig, who had denied to the professors of the "schools" the attribute of philosopher, had met in Cohen one whom "without mockery" he would call a philosopher.[28]

But Cohen was not only a philosopher in the new sense that Rosenzweig demanded as the only true form of post-Hegelian philosophy. He was a Jew, and—what must have evoked a deep response on the part of Rosenzweig—he was a Jew who from the "world" had returned to the fold. He had found the "center of his being." Now he wanted to serve his people. In his intro-

[27] *Briefe*, p. 305.
[28] Letter No. 9; *Kl. Schr.*, p. 291. [For a critical evaluation of Rosenzweig's view of Cohen see now the author's essay "Hermann Cohens Begriff der Korrelation," *In Zwei Welten, Siegfried Moses zum Fünfundsiebzigsten Geburtstag*, ed. by Hans Tramer (Tel-Aviv, 1962) pp. 377–99.]

duction to Hermann Cohen's *Jüdische Schriften* (1923)—the great memorial to his master—Rosenzweig recorded some of the things that Cohen had said to him in private conversation. They must have struck him deeply, because he himself had just discovered the center of his own life in Judaism. Cohen was pleading at that time for the establishment of a chair for Jewish philosophy at one of the German universities.[29] Rosenzweig was thrilled with the idea. In one of his letters from the war—written at the time of the correspondence—he emphasized its importance for the spiritual renewal of Judaism. He felt that he could give of his best if such a post were offered to him.[30] All his literary plans receded into the background before the deeper concern of his new life: his Judaism.

Yet the question of "Judaism and Christianity" still occupied his mind. The lectures that Cohen held in 1913–14 gave him a living answer to this problem. He found in Cohen an uncompromising Jew who insisted on the fundamental differences between Judaism and Christianity. Rosenzweig recorded some of the striking utterances made by Cohen in the course of the lectures that his "happy ears were privileged to hear":[31] "God be what He be, but He must be One"; "On this point we cannot come to an understanding with Christianity"; the unity of God, "the most abstract idea, . . . for whose sake we are killed all the day" (Psalms 44:22); "Balaam's word of the 'people that shall dwell alone' (Numbers 23:9), the civilized world cannot comprehend it"; "The whole of Nature, the model of art, is opened up in the Second Commandment—and sealed. This is something for which the world has never forgiven us"; "The Greek spirit, that is the type of the scientific mind, looks for mediation, as they call it, between God and man. To this Greek charm the Jew Philo and his Logos fell a victim"; "Had Philo not invented the Logos, no Jew would ever have fallen away from God."[32] Sometimes it was only a gesture, a single word, and one could feel the eruptive power of his personality. When Rosenzweig once says that the

[29] *Kleinere Schriften*, p. 323.
[30] *Briefe*, p. 92.
[31] *Kleinere Schriften*, p. 337.
[32] *Ibid.*, pp. 337, 340–41.

Jewish attitude "might sometime be expressed in a gesture, but hardly perhaps in words",[33] Hermann Cohen stands before his mind; and many a passage in these letters[34] could hardly have been written by Rosenzweig without the experience of Hermann Cohen, the fighter and the Jew.

The war broke out. The world was in a fever of excitement. Yet Rosenzweig was not too deeply affected by it. As he confessed in a letter to Hans Ehrenberg, dated October, 1916:

> The war itself has not caused any break in my inner life. In 1913 I had experienced so much that the year 1914 would have had to produce nothing short of the world's final collapse to make any impression on me . . . . Thus I have not experienced the war. . . . I carry my life through this war like Cervantes his poem.[35]

This should not be taken as an indication of apathy but rather of a profound concentration of his mind on the future task of his life, which was to have its center, not in the outside world with its changing events, but in the midst of his people.

Rosenstock he had met again in the summer of 1914, but the subject that had united and divided them was not touched upon. Rosenzweig tried to evade a new discussion; he felt himself not yet mature enough to face his former opponent. Though he was firmly established in his new philosophy and theology, he realized that he had still to grow, and that his life had still to be shaped according to his new insight, before he could meet Rosenstock as an "accomplished fact." And yet, secretly, he was waiting for that final discussion in which he was to meet him as a Jew and secure his recognition as a Jew. It was Rosenstock who broke the silence. During a short stay in Kassel, where he enjoyed the hospitality of Rosenzweig's parents and occupied his friend's room, he wrote to him. The letter started a correspondence in which both their human relationship and the objective problem of the relationship of the two faiths found expression. The two correspondents were then on active service in the army. Some of the letters were written from the trenches and under enemy

[33] See Letter No. 9.
[34] See Letter No. 11.
[35] *Briefe*, p. 123.

fire. The correspondence began in May, 1916. In October, Rosenzweig reported to Rudolf Ehrenberg:

I am having a correspondence with Rosenstock which is not an easy thing for me; we have not yet got over the initial stage, and it proves to be very bad that since that night's conversation in 1913 . . . I have not really spoken to him; as a matter of fact, I could not have done it, because I had to continue the discussion with his ghost of that night.[36]

On December 24 the correspondence had been completed, and Rosenzweig was able to write, again to Rudolf Ehrenberg:

The real adventure and achievement of the last few months was for me my correspondence with Rosenstock. You will read it one day. You know (or should be able to know) that I expected, dreaded, and postponed the inevitable second discussion with him since November, 1913. It was to be the test of my new life. . . . Now the task is completed.[37]

The correspondence was not only a great document of their renewed friendship, but it was of decisive influence on their future work. It helped them to clarify their ideas and to cast them into their final form. "Without Eugen I would never have written *The Star of Redemption*," Rosenzweig confessed later.[38] There are two things in particular that Rosenzweig owed to this correspondence. In the first place, it deepened his conception of revelation. The question that had worried him was: Is it possible, and *how* is it possible, to define revelation as distinct and distinguishable from any expression or form of the natural mind? All his endeavors in this respect had resulted in merely historical, not logical, distinctions.[39] His correspondence with Rosenstock gave him an opportunity to ask his friend point blank to explain to him his present idea of the relation between nature and revelation.[40] Rosenstock's answer was: revelation means orientation. After revelation there exists a real Above and Below in the world,

[36] *Ibid.*, p. 121.
[37] *Ibid.*, p. 143.
[38] "Das neue Denken" (see note 4 above).
[39] *Kleinere Schriften*, p. 357.
[40] *Briefe*, p. 53.

and a real Before and Hereafter in time. In the "natural" world and in "natural" time the point where I happen to be is the center of the universe; in the space-time world of revelation the center is fixed, and my movements and changes do not alter it. Rosenzweig felt this was an idea of stupendous simplicity and productivity.[41] Though he did not accept it as a final solution to his problem, it was certainly of great help to him. His own "point of Archimedes," which enabled him to write *The Star of Redemption*, he found a year later, in October, 1917.[42]

There is another point that deserves mentioning. In the correspondence one finds an exposition of Rosenstock's "philosophy in the form of a calendar," as illustrated by his charts of the year. It may strike one as rather queer and arbitrary. But it should be taken simply as the first imaginative suggestion of an idea that he developed with a certain fruitfulness in his *Out of Revolution*.[43] There he tries a way of writing the history of Europe in the light of its festivals, its holidays and holy-days, its celebrations of national revolutions; for a historical event is not a mere event but something taken up out of the mere passage of time into the experience of a people. The calendar may therefore be taken as a symptom of a people's corporate memory, its celebration of the crucial moments in its experience, its sense of what is important or significant. The "present," as a concrete moment in time, must be experienced as an intersection of four "calendars." Rosenstock symbolized it as a cross in which the "present" is the point of intersection, and the four ends represent the course of nature, the course of "secular history," the course of "sacred" (the church's) history, and one's private calendar of inner development.

Rosenzweig seems to have accepted this idea. In his *Star of Redemption* the calendars of the synagogue and the church—those "two eternal dial plates under the weekly and annual pointer of ever-renewed Time"[44]—play an integral part. But the relation of the sacred calendar to the courses of nature, history,

[41] *Kleinere Schriften*, p. 359.
[42] Cf. *ibid.*, p. 357.
[43] New York: William Morrow & Co., 1938.
[44] *Kl. Schr.*, p. 392.

and man is a different one. Its symbol is not the Cross with its four points, but the Jewish Star of David with its six points formed by the intersection of two triangles, of which God, World, and Man form the apexes of one; Creation, Revelation, and Redemption of the other. The three elements of reality, i.e., God, World, and Man, appear each in three different qualities: God is Creator, Revealer, and Redeemer. Man is a natural being (part of creation); the receiver of Revelation (Priest and Prophet); the agent of Redemption (the holy work of the Saint). The World is Creation (Natural law, *civitas mundi*); the place of Revelation (community of the believers); the place of the accomplished Redemption (Messianic Day, *civitas Dei*).

Rosenzweig's influence on Rosenstock can be clearly seen in the chapter on the French Revolution and the emancipation of the Jews in the latter's book *Out of Revolution*.[45] There paganism and Judaism are interpreted as the Alpha and Omega of history:

God's Alpha was lived by the Gentiles, and God's Omega is embodied in the Jews. . . . The Jews represent the end of human history before its actual end. Without them pagan history would not only have had no goal, but would have gotten nowhere. The pagans represent the eternal new beginnings of history, and without them history would never have acquired any shape or form or beauty or fulfillment or attainment."[46]

Between Jews and pagans stands Christianity as the mediator: "The true Christians can preach the Gospel among the Gentiles. They are the rays sent out from this central fire [i.e., Judaism], which actually transform the world. As coals in the heart of fire, the Jews are prisoners of God."[47] The "periodical persecutions of the Jews" represent a succession of attempts on the part of the Gentiles "to throw off the yoke which joins Alpha and Omega."[48]

In the correspondence Rosenstock had still refused to recog-

[45] *Out of Revolution*, pp. 216–17.
[46] *Ibid.*, p. 225.
[47] *Ibid.*, p. 221.
[48] *Ibid.*, p. 226.

nize in Christianity the "Judaizing of the pagans."[49] The year 1789, which to Rosenzweig signified the final triumph of revelation in the world and the beginning of a new era in history—the dawn of the Johannine age—was considered by Rosenstock in just the reverse sense as the "mightiest outbreak" of the natural, i.e., pagan, mind.[50] Since 1789, he felt, paganism had become dominant even in the churches. He pointed to Adolf von Harnack as the symbol of the paganizing of Christianity, its abandonment of faith in revelation, and its belief in the achievements of the natural mind. Rosenzweig replied that the modern nationalism of the peoples are not to be confounded with the paganism of the ἔθνη of antiquity. "For nationalism not merely expresses the peoples' belief that they come *from* God (that, as you rightly say, the pagans also believe), but that they go *to* God." This means "the complete Christianizing of the conception of a people," though "not yet the Christianizing of the peoples themselves." Israel was still the only people in the world in whom revelation was a reality.[51] Rosenstock still disagreed. He felt that modern nationalism was not a Christianizing of the conception of the people but meant that the nations had adopted the idea of the Roman Empire. Modern nationalism was but a rebirth of pagan imperialism.[52]

In *Out of Revolution* Rosenstock finally accepted Rosenzweig's view that 1789 meant the Christianizing of the idea of nations and thus the triumph of Judaism. The "great idea of humanity as conceived by the French Revolution . . . had discovered man behind men, nature behind nations, Adam behind Shem, Ham and Japhet, and the great identity of all men behind creed, faith, colour and race."[53] Through the act of the emancipation of the Jews, the nations are inoculated with the Jewish promise. "By the addition of the element of Omega, the chosen people of God, the 'Alphaic' nations have acquired one touch of finality and predestination."[54] "Messianism, originally limited to

[49] See Letter No. 12.
[50] See Letter No. 12.
[51] See Letter No. 15.
[52] See Letter No. 16.
[53] *Out of Revolution*, p. 235.
[54] *Ibid.*, p. 236.

the Jews, later communicated to the heathen by the Church, is transferred by the European nationalism born in 1789 to the nations in general, which now enter upon a common race of *messianic nationalism.*"[55] Rosenstock is confident that "the admixture of the Jews, who can never be treated as pagans, secures the nation from backsliding and mistaking mere existence for growth, inheritance for heritage, alpha for omega."[56]

This is clearly Rosenzweig's idea of the Johannine epoch. But Rosenzweig died in 1929, at the last moment when it was still possible to ignore the rising tide of the new paganism, which Rosenstock seems to have forecast in these letters.[57] Rosenstock's faith in the irreversible messianic course of history, "in spite of Hitlerism,"[58] is all the more remarkable. In the light of his theology the present persecutions of the Jews must be interpreted as another, perhaps final, attempt on the part of the Gentiles to throw off the yoke that joins Alpha and Omega, the first and the last things. In trying to exterminate the Jewish people, the new paganism wants to eradicate the messianic element from history.

Rosenstock felt certain that by the absorption of the Jews the modern nations had become immune against a return to paganism. His confidence in the decisive victory of revelation in 1789 led him to believe that there was no further necessity for the continued existence of Israel as a visible synagogue. He felt that we were living in a new spiritual era in which the functions of Gentiles, Christians, and Jews were no longer invested in a visible race, a visible clergy, and a visible Israel. "In the future the character and the function of a man can no longer be judged by the outward signs of race, creed, or country. He has to choose for himself."[59] The events of recent years are certainly not likely to confirm this view. The nations are far from being transformed into the messianic kingdom that would allow them to disregard the visible manifestations of church and synagogue. They are still in danger of backsliding into paganism. The functions of

---

[55] *Ibid.*
[56] *Ibid.*
[57] See Letter No. 16.
[58] *Out of Revolution*, p. 237.
[59] *Ibid.*

church and synagogue have not come to an end. Israel has to remain alive in order to send out the "Rays from the heart of the fire" until the day in which "God is One and His Name One."

The Letters of Franz Rosenzweig
and Eugen Rosenstock-Huessy
by Dorothy M. Emmet*

* Reprinted, with minor editorial revisions, from *The Journal of Religion* (October, 1945), by permission of the University of Chicago Press and Miss Emmet, now Samuel Hall Professor of Philosophy, Emerita, University of Manchester, England. In introducing Miss Emmet's article to readers of the *Journal*, the editor commented, in part:

"The author submitted the paper to Dr. Rosenstock-Huessy. Rather than introduce comments into the paper, he refers readers of it to his article in our April issue of this year: 'Hitler and Israel, or On Prayer,' for fuller understanding of the deeper issues involved in the correspondence. . . .

"The correspondence in the present selection inevitably presents Dr. Rosenstock-Huessy largely in the role of a foil to Rosenzweig. The latter's notable interpretation of Judaism is set in a high light. There may be in consequence some obscuring of the context of Dr. Rosenstock-Huessy's thought at the time and particularly in his priority in exploring what later became so significant in the work of Martin Buber, namely, the 'I–Thou' philosophy. [*N.B.*: See the *"Editor's note"* immediately following Miss Emmet's essay, on p. 69.] Particular light on the setting of the correspondence is suggested by Dr. Rosenstock-Huessy in a series of observations addressed to the editor. 'We both,' he says, 'were nearly drowned by a third force, neither Christian nor Jewish, the spirit of nineteenth-century positivism. Our brotherhood consisted in our, both of us, emerging in vigorous swimming from the abyss of this faithless, godless "world" without "star, love, Fortune." So our negation we had in common; and with regard to this negation, I was in the lead. With regard to the goal, we were in disagreement.'

"Dr. Rosenstock-Huessy, moreover, makes [it] clear that the correspondence has a bearing beyond that of the particular situation in 1917 when 'they treated Judaism and Christianity as simple unities which, in fact, nowhere are found in the realities of our day, with the innumerable divisions of faith and creed inside the religious denominations. I, for my part, feel that this was the chrysalis of a more rational and more scientific approach to the eternal features which, out of Judaism, Christianity and, third, out of

48

In a recent article in the *Journal of Religion* (October, 1944), Dr. Altmann told the story of the inner development of the Jewish writer Franz Rosenzweig as an introduction to his correspondence with the Christian philosopher-historian, Eugen Rosenstock. He thus gave the background of the correspondence and spoke of the influence it was to have on the future work of the two men. The letters were written in 1916, when the two correspondents were on active service: Rosenstock as an officer on the Western Front (except for a short period in Kassel), and Rosenzweig as a noncommissioned officer in an antiballoon battery in Macedonia. Written under war conditions, they sense a spiritual situation of which we are now acutely aware: the breaking-up of the European tradition as it has come down to us from Greeks and Romans, Jews and Christians, and the emergence of a strange new world of races and nations prepared to forget its inheritance. What do Judaism and Christianity mean in this "post-European" world and what do they mean in relation to each other? In these letters we see Rosenzweig and Rosenstock wrestling with their individual solutions to this question. They confront each other, as Dr. Altmann has said, not as a Jew and a Christian but as two men who had come to define their own standpoints to themselves as well as to each other through a profoundly sincere adventure in communication.

Let us now turn to the chapter in this adventure represented by the correspondence. Dr. Altmann has shown how, as a result of his contact with Rosenstock, Rosenzweig had come near to becoming a Christian, and then had seen that for him the decision must lie not for Christianity but for a positive identification of himself with the Jewish faith of his people. He had not yet been able to speak of this development to Rosenstock. The opportun-

---

Greek Humanism, must be carried over into a future in which we all will have to have access to all three positions.' He has in mind here the time *future* of the Jew, the time *past*, or *archè*, of the Greek (which he associates with Heidegger), and the time *present*, the Today, of the Christian which 'marries' the other two. 'All three, then, master time. And of the mastery of time, our correspondence tried to give an account, with a sincerity which only exists on the three levels of Greek, Jewish, and Christian approach to the one question which forces us to think at all: What is time, temporality, secularity, mortality, flux? Because here alone we face death.' "

ity came with the present correspondence, opened by Rosenstock when he was staying with Rosenzweig's parents in their home in Kassel during a period of training as an officer in the army. He wrote introducing himself in what he thought would surprise his friend as a new role, no longer that of "jurist-historian" but that of "philosopher." But this was no surprise to Rosenzweig. "You have never—I mean to say during the last few years—been to me anything other than a philosopher. I have always felt that the jurist and the historian were only incidental." All the same, Rosenzweig complains, he wants not mere hints but a sample of this "philosophy."

In spite of a hint that he was about to embark upon a system, Rosenstock's philosophy was not systematic in the traditional sense. From the "samples" with which he supplied his friend we gather that it was an attempt to read human history in terms of the "calendars" of different forms of experience. For "history" is no mere dead record of events; it is the interpretative record of events that have been taken up into the experience of a people, or, as autobiography, into a personal experience. Rosenstock was seeking to read the experience of the peoples of Europe by taking their calendar for guide, with their festivals, holidays, and holy days. He was later to follow out this idea in his book *Out of Revolution*.[1] Here he sketches the outline of this method to Rosenzweig. The movement of time, he suggests, acquires significance for us in the intersection of a fourfold calendar: the calendar of the course of nature; that of world history; that of the sacred history of the church; and one's own private calendar of inner development.

Such a novel way of philosophizing struck a sympathetic chord in Rosenzweig; though, when Rosenstock took it to the length of trying to give symbolic meanings to different months, we suspect that he thought that his friend was letting his imagination run away with him. At any rate, when later on Rosenstock leaves several letters unanswered, he gently asks him whether November stands for "Forgetfulness." But he, too, was seeing

[1] New York: William Morrow & Co., 1938. [N.B.: Paperback reprint available through Argo Books, Inc., Box 283, Norwich, Vt. 05055.—*publisher's note.*]

that the extent to which the development of a philosopher's thinking is related to the inner form of his own mind needed to be more clearly acknowledged than it had been in the philosophy of the schools. Hegel had, in principle if not in actual execution, said the last word in the type of philosophy that claimed to be the construction of a universal system by a mind that could look on itself not merely as that of a human thinker but as an embodiment of "consciousness in general." So since Hegel, he says,[2] there have been only learned "doctors" or "professors" of philosophy, except for those who have been feeling after a new method of thinking.

We may observe in passing that this awareness of a break with the older conception of metaphysics has led to a radical repudiation of philosophy and philosophical method in any sense of the term in circles touched by the Barthian theological revival, more particularly on the continent of Europe. The break has been less violent in England and America, perhaps because our philosophy has never been as absolute in its claims, whether positive or negative, as that of the German schools, especially the schools of German Idealism; even Idealism in England and America has been Idealism in a more modest vein. It is therefore the more significant that Rosenzweig himself did not so succumb to theology as to make a complete break with philosophy; throughout these letters, and in *The Star of Redemption*, he remained conscious of himself as a philosopher. In one of these letters[3] he writes of a book by Karl Heim:[4] "Heim's weakness . . . as that of his whole circle, is that the history of philosophy ceases for him with Kant, and as an alternative to the Idealists, he knows only the specialist dogmatic theologians of the nineteenth century, and so he does not ask himself: How would it be if philosophy itself were to take the paradox as its basis?" Presumably he means by the "paradox" the word as Kierkegaard used it; the question of how

[2] See Letter No. 2.
[3] See Letter No. 11.
[4] Karl Heim, professor of theology in Münster and, from 1920, Tübingen; author of *Der evangelische Glaube und das Denken der Gegenwart* (Berlin, 1931–), the first volume of which (*Glaube und Denken*) was translated into English under the title *God Transcendent* (New York, 1936).

general and universal truth can be expressed in terms of existence, which is always historical and individual. But while Kierkegaard's thought remains that of the solitary individual, and can be perverse for all its penetration, Rosenzweig and Rosenstock have grasped how an individual comes to reach his own standpoint by exposing himself to encounter with others at a sufficiently profound level. Rosenzweig renounces therefore not philosophy but the pretensions of the Hegelian Idealist philosophy. Instead of an attempt at a universal world system, we must have attempts at systems wrought out through "one's inner form of life"; and "this personal character must not (as Hegel still believed in the *Phenomenology*) be overcome in order that the system may follow from it, but because it is being purified step by step, the system seen from the point of view of the author is his way to salvation."[5] A system is therefore the clarification of a Weltanschauung, an outlook on life of a thinker who is not "consciousness in general" but a human being himself immersed in the process of living.

Rosenzweig was very conscious, however, that he was not yet ready to express what he might have to say as a philosopher. He was conscious of having broken with his former style in these studies. Before he could write again, he had to come to terms with himself as a Jew, and he knew it. He also knew that, until he had done so, he could not meet Rosenstock again as one who was both his spiritual antithesis and his alter ego. "We were thesis and antithesis in Leipzig[6] (but not on a level, because I was your pupil). What we are now, *I don't know*, be it only because I don't know myself definitely as an –ologist or an –osopher. On the whole I now know less than I did before; I am waiting."[7]

Meanwhile, while waiting, "simple industry" may help. He wants to study some church history in the Fathers and Scholastics and asks Rosenstock, as a specialist, for advice about books. The reply suggests that Rosenstock was still rather more of the specialist and scholar than the experienced soldier. He writes that unfortunately the Leonine Edition of St. Thomas Aquinas

[5] See Letter No. 7.
[6] See Altmann, pp. 31–32 above.
[7] See Letter No. 4.

is temporarily unobtainable because it is published in Italy, but he consoles him by saying that "the early Scholastics are comparatively cheap in Migne's *Patrologia*; you can get a big volume of a thousand pages for from 10 to 14 marks."[8] This calls out the rueful reply from Rosenzweig in his anti-aircraft battery in Macedonia: "Your recommending Migne has moved me to tears—one volume in each trouser pocket, one tied up in the tail of my battle charger, two more in my saddle bags—but no, the beasts aren't getting any more oats—vanish dream!"[9]

How far the two friends had moved from understanding each other's present state of mind was revealed when Rosenstock began a letter: "Dear Fellow Jew + post-Christum natum + post-Hegel mortuum!"[10] That Rosenstock should count himself a Jew too only shows, says Rosenzweig, how little he knows about it. "I must say it, however reluctantly. You are directly hindering me from treating my Judaism in the first person, in that you call yourself a Jew too. That is to me equally intolerable, emotionally and intellectually." Rosenstock had cited the unwritten saying of Jesus connected with Luke 6:5, that a man who breaks the Sabbath is blessed if he knows what he is doing, but cursed if he does not know—probably as an allusion to a man's freedom to choose his faith. He himself had joined the church; but, says Rosenzweig, "any sense of identification with Judaism can only be yours in a theoretical retrospect, not in the reality of your life before you became a Christian; and I know this life now because I know your parent's home." He goes on to say that an emancipated Jew, with no roots in the life of his people, does not understand how deeply the "stubbornness of the Jews" enters both into Christian and into Jewish theology. Such a one is neither a Jew to whom the preaching of the Cross is a stumbling block nor a pagan philosopher to whom it is foolishness; he is a bare individual without conscious tradition, and he can take the world in all innocence for a *mundus naturaliter Christianus*.[11]

Rosenstock is puzzled by this emphatic insistence on the

8 See Letter No. 8.
9 See Letter No. 9.
10 See Letter No. 8.
11 See Letter No. 9.

"separateness" and "stubbornness" of the Jews, coming as it does from Rosenzweig, whom he had known first as a liberal intellectual and then as a near Christian. He can see why the *church* may have needed to see the Jews in this way.

> The Jews are so much the chosen people and the Old Testament so much the book of the law of the Father, just as the New Testament is the book of the love of the children (Abraham and Christ, sacrifice the two poles, on the one hand the Father, on the other, the Son), that altogether the church needs "its" Jews to strengthen its own truth. The stubbornness of the Jews is, so to speak, a Christian dogma. But is it, can it, also be a Jewish one? That is the fence that I do not see you taking . . .[12]

Of himself he can say:

> In respect of part of me, I presume to judge myself as pre-Christian Jewish material. In my capacity for suffering and in my craving for it, the Jew comes out. I forge together German and Jewish gifts and possessions in my attempt to become a Christian. This is my quite uncritical view of myself. And, as I said before, my attitude to you remains quite incomprehensible to me; it is not indifferent and yet tolerant, and I am content to ask myself, with Cyrano: "Que diable allait-il faire dans cette galère?" (What the devil was he going to do on that galley?)[13]

The "galley" is, of course, Judaism, and Rosenzweig was quick to take up the metaphor. But he would not have felt himself ready to explain his presence in the galley to his friend had not the course of events forced him to do so.

> When you were in Berlin in the spring . . . I didn't feel myself strong enough, not indeed physically, but spiritually, to challenge you all over again (since it would only have been done as a challenge, and will so be done again); to my mind I was not actual enough, not tested enough, not enough on the spot, and to me there would have been no point in a merely theoretical controversy. Formerly, I had confronted you as a point of view, as an objective fact, and you were the first to summon me to an analysis of myself, and thereby you cast me down. I should have liked to wait until I

---

[12] See Letter No. 10.
[13] See Letter No. 10.

could again confront you as a *fait accompli*. Till then we could have kept our guest rooms ready for each other, and put some little cheap flowers in them as a token of our feeling for one another. That does, and would have done.

"Then the war came." And with it came a time of waiting against one's will, a chasm that one does not make artificially for oneself, but which was opened blindly in every life; and now it is no longer any good to wait deliberately; fate is now so calmly patient with individuals (from indifference towards them, because it has its hands full with nations), that we individuals ought just now to be impatient, unless we want simply to go to sleep (for fate certainly won't wake us up now). So now we are talking to each other theoretically *faute de mieux*. But for that reason everything that we say to each other is incomplete, not incomplete like the flow of life which completes itself anew in every moment, but full of static incompletenesses, full of distortions.[14]

How the "stubbornness of the Jews" became a Christian dogma Rosenzweig explains from his reading of church history. The church, appealing against the Marcionites to the teaching of Paul, both established the Old Testament in the canon and at the same time believed that she was following Paul in holding that the Jews would remain cast out until the fullness of the Gentiles had been gathered in.

But could this same idea (that of the stubbornness of the Jews) also be a Jewish dogma? Yes, it could be, and in fact it is. But this Jewish consciousness of being rejected has quite a different place in our dogmatic system, and would correspond to a Christian consciousness of being chosen to rule, a consciousness that is in fact present beyond any doubt. The whole religious interpretation of the significance of the year 70 is tuned to this note. But the parallel that you are looking for is something entirely different; a dogma of Judaism about its relation to the Church must correspond to the dogma of the Church about its relation to Judaism. And this you know only in the form of the modern liberal-Jewish theory of the "daughter religion" that gradually educates the world for Judaism. But this theory actually springs from the classical period in the formation of Jewish dogma—from the Jewish high scholasticism which, in point of time and in content, forms a mean between

[14] See Letter No. 11.

55

Christian and Arabian scholasticism (al-Ghazali–Maimonides–Thomas Aquinas). For it was only then that we had a fixing of dogma, and that corresponds with the different position that intellectual conceptions of faith hold with us and with you. In the period when you were developing dogma, we were creating our canon law, and vice versa. There is a subtle connection running all through. For instance, when you were systematizing dogma, we were systematizing law; with you the mystical view of dogma followed its definition, while with us the mystical view preceded definition, etc., etc. This relation is rooted in the final difference between the two faiths.

Indeed with us, too, this theory [of the daughter religion] is not part of the substance of our dogma; with us, too, it was not formed from the content of the religious consciousness but belongs only to a second stratum, a stratum of learning concerning dogma. The theory of the daughter religion is found in the clearest form in both of the great scholastics. Beyond this, it is found, not as dogma but as a mystical idea . . . in the literature of the old Synagogue, and likewise in the Talmudic period. . . .[15]

One such legend tells that "the Messiah was born exactly at the moment when the Temple was destroyed; but when he was born the winds blew him forth from the bosom of his mother. And now he wanders unknown among the peoples, and when he has wandered through them all, then the time of our redemption has come." Another is the saying of the great scholastic Yehudah ha-Levi: Christianity is the tree which grows from the seed of Judaism and overshadows the earth; but the fruit of the tree must contain the seed again, and nobody notices that who merely sees the tree. In some such sense there is a Jewish dogma,[16] "just as Judaism as both the stubborn origin and last convert is a Christian dogma."[17]

"But what does that mean for me?" asks Rosenzweig. What does this Jewish dogma mean for the Jews? And what does the

[15] See Letter No. 11.

[16] That is, that Christianity exists to spread the knowledge of the biblical God throughout the nations, thereby preparing them for Judaism in the days of the Messiah.

[17] See Letter No. 11.

corresponding Christian dogma mean to contemporary Christians, who have forgotten its theological roots?

The answer is already on the point of my pen—that it was not here a matter of theoretical awareness, but whether there was a continual realization of this theological idea by taking it seriously in actual practice. This practical way in which the theological idea of the stubbornness of the Jew works itself out, is *hatred of the Jews*.[18]

On the Jewish side the corresponding outcome of their dogma is the *pride of the Jews*.

This is hard to describe to a stranger. What you see of it appears to you silly and petty, just as it is almost impossible for the Jew to see and judge anti-Semitism by anything but its vulgar and stupid expressions. But (I must say again, *believe me*) its metaphysical basis is, as I have said, the three articles: (1) that we have the truth; (2) that we are at the goal; and (3) that any and every Jew feels in the depths of his soul that the Christian relation to God, and so in a sense their religion, is particularly and extremely pitiful, poverty-stricken, and ceremonious; namely, that as a Christian one has to learn from someone else, whoever he may be, to call God "our Father." To the Jew that God is our Father is the first and most self-evident fact—and what need is there for a third person between me and my Father in Heaven? That is no discovery of modern apologetics but the simplest Jewish instinct, a mixture of failure to understand and pitying contempt.

These are the two points of view, both narrow and limited just as points of view, and so in theory both can be surpassed; one can understand why the Jew can afford his unmediated closeness to God and why the Christian may not, and one can also understand how the Jew must pay for this blessing.[19]

[18] See Letter No. 11. Dr. J. W. Parkes has shown in his study, *The Conflict of the Church and the Synagogue* (London, 1934), to what an extent anti-Semitism in patristic and medieval times grew out of the theological conception of the "stubbornness of the Jews," who were held to have forfeited their promises to the new Israel. This conception of the collective guilt of a people provided Christians with a scapegoat, "the Jews"; and it has remained in this form even where its theological roots have been forgotten or repudiated.

[19] See Letter No. 11.

Part of the price which the synagogue must pay is that she carries a broken staff and wears bandages over her eyes. This symbolism, taken from the medieval sculptured figures of the church and the synagogue, such as those in the cathedral at Bamberg, is a recurrent motif in Rosenzweig's letters. He had used it in the letter to Rudolf Ehrenberg in which he explained his decision to become a Jew.[20] The church, with the crown on her head and the scepter in her hand, has "her eyes open to the world, a fighter sure of victory." But the synagogue, with the bandage over her eyes, can only "see with the prophetic eye of inner vision the last and most distant things." Hence the extreme nature of life in Judaism, the separating and exclusive nature of its practice. It preserves the inner integrity of Jewish life. And Rosenzweig himself, to the question, "What are you doing in that galley?" can only answer that he is no "convert"; it is his birthright.

Have I only been thrown into the galley? Is it not *my* ship? You have become acquainted with me on land, but you have scarcely noticed that my ship lies in harbor and that I spend more time than is necessary in sailors' taverns,[21] and therefore you could well ask what business I have on the ship. And for you really to believe that it is my ship, and that I therefore belong to it (*pour faire quoi? y vivre et y mourir*)—for you really to believe me will only be possible if the voyage is once more free and I launch out. Or only when we meet out on the open sea? You might![22]

So the Jewish form of the dogma of the stubbornness of the Jews is the pride of the Jews in their election. Yes, says Rosenstock; and it is precisely from this pride that Christianity redeems us.

That from which Christ redeems is exactly the boundless naïve pride of the Jew, which you yourself exhibit. In contrast to the peoples talking the 372 languages of Babel, this pride was and is well founded, and therefore the Jews were separated and chosen out of all the peoples of the earth, until the destruction of the Temple. But Christianity redeems the individual from family and people through the new unity of sinners, all who are weary and heavy laden. That is

[20] *Briefe*, p. 71; cf. Altmann, pp. 32–33, 37.
[21] That is, presumably, our common cultural life.
[22] See Letter No. 11.

Christianity, and its bond is equal need. My brain is going on strike, and I am getting stupid. I only know that I should like to wax eloquent over *peccatum originale* and *superbia judaica*, but the machine has run dry. I am so exhausted that you must do with this. I feel as though I were always writing the same thing. My love to you. Fortunately you do not know what you do. Your E. R.[23]

Renewing the same theme, Rosenstock notes that, while for the Christian some measure of implication and hence compromise with the life of the world is seen as inevitable and as part of the "taking up of the Cross" to which he is called, for the Jew any such implication is fatal to his separateness. So what about the life of modern Jews? "F.R. as a volunteer in the army? Where is there the metaphysics of the seed of Abraham?" The synagogue has not faced this question of living in the world, and hence, says Rosenstock, her sterility. "The teachings and events, which through the continuous stimulus of Christianity have changed the face of the earth during the last thousand years, have as their opposite numbers in Judaism a couple of distinguished names, pressed into the service of the pride of the Synagogue, and otherwise nothing."[24]

Rosenstock then picks up again the motif of the contrast of Abraham's sacrifice and Christ's sacrifice, the two archetypal sacrifices which he had said represented the "poles" of the two religions. (We may recall how Genesis, chap. 22, is read as the first lesson on Good Friday in the ecclesiastical lectionaries.) "Abraham," he says, "sacrifices his son; in the New Testament he who brings the covenant with God sacrifices himself. That is the whole difference . . . Abraham sacrifices what he has, Christ what he is." And then follows an outburst, which only the sincerity of the correspondence makes possible, in which Rosenstock attacks the exclusiveness of the Jew's faith in his election. Perhaps (though the connection is not stated) the reference to the two sacrifices leads to this outburst because Rosenstock sees the story of Abraham and Isaac as expressing the idea of the reestablishment of Israel as the possessors of the covenant; whereas he looks on the story of Christ's self sacrifice as expressing the

[23] See Letter No. 12.
[24] See Letter No. 13.

readiness of the chosen one to die in order that the covenant might be universalized for all mankind. So he inveighs in no measured language against the exclusiveness of the Jewish claims.

The Synagogue has been talking for two thousand years about what she had, because she really has absolutely nothing; but she does not experience and will, therefore, not experience what she is. She portrays the curse of self-assurance, of pride in her nobility, and thoughtless indifference towards the law of growth of the united universe, the "Peace on earth to all men in whom he is well pleased." That new humanity from universal need and sin, that ever newly born *corpus christianum* of all men of good will—that being called out from all people—is something of which she knows nothing. She knows an original union in blood, that of the chosen people, but no final becoming united of all the children of the Father. The Jews have the saying that all men will come to Jerusalem to pray, and they always crucify again the one who came to make the word true. In appearance they wait upon the word of the Lord, but they have grown through and through so far away from revelation that they do everything they can to hinder its reality. With all the power of their being they set themselves against their own promises. They are the image on earth of Lucifer, the highest of the angels, elect of God, who wanted to keep God's gift for himself as a dominion in his own right, and fell. So Israel stands upon its own inalienable right. This naïve way of thinking that one has won inalienable rights in perpetuity against God, which by nature remain for posterity as properties inherited by bequest, is the relic of blind antiquity in Judaism. . . .

But I will not allow any *rabies theologica* to come in. I know that Israel will survive all the peoples, but you have no aptitude for theology, for the search for truth, any more than for beauty. Ye shall make for yourselves no graven image. At this cost the eternal Jew is allowed to live. Because he holds on to life in such an unlimited way, it is granted to him. . . . In order that Israel may live, the individual Jew depends on his success, on the number of his children. He is a paragraph of the Law. *C'est tout.* You may well believe that you have a ship of your own. But you have no idea of the sea or you would not talk like that. You know no shipwreck; you cannot go astray, you see God with constant clarity, and so you need no mediator, who looks at you when you can no longer look out over the edge of the world, and are frustrated in failure. You do not know that the world is movement and change. The Christian says there are day and night. You are so moonstruck that you take the sight of night for the only sight there is, and take the minimum of light, the night, for the all-inclusive idea that embraces day and night! *Lasciate ogni speranza* . . .[25]

This outburst reached Rosenzweig on a morning on which he says he had just learned by bitter experience (no doubt by barking his shins) that Rosewood (= Rosenstock) is the hardest wood that there is.

Yes indeed, here is the real tough Rosenstock, and now I no longer have any difficulty in writing to you. You have given me a much more impersonal answer than I asked for. In many ways so impersonal that I asked myself this morning: Haven't I really written all this before, for him to write it to me?
You are quite right in everything you say in your *rabies theologica*. I really mean, you must know that I know all that. And that I also know that you have to see Judaism like that. I was only puzzled that right at the beginning of our correspondence you talked differently from the way in which you do now. Nevertheless, there is a point beyond which neither Christian rabies, nor Jewish rabulistic[26] should go, however much they both would like to do so once they have got into their stride. For you may curse, you may swear, you may scratch yourself as much as you like, you won't get rid of us, we are the louse in your fur. . . . We are the internal foe; don't mix us up with the external one! Our enmity may have to be bitterer than any enmity for the external foe, but all the same—we and you are within the same frontiers, in the same kingdom.[27]

That is to say, in the realm of the spirit Rosenzweig sees the two faiths both as mutually exclusive and yet as complementary. In a poem by Rosenstock written after this there occurs the phrase "Enemies in Space, brethren in Time."
Rosenzweig returns to the Jew's faith in his "election." Even today when, as Rosenstock had pointed out, every nation looks

[25] See Letter No. 13.
[26] Sophistry.
[27] See Letter No. 15.

on itself in some way as a "chosen people," the Jewish election remains something unique in its "peculiar pride or peculiar modesty." It is anything but naïve; it is rooted in the present reality of its faith.

Now that I want to continue, I find that everything that I want to write is something which I can't express to you. For now I would have to show you Judaism from within, that is, be able to show it to you in a hymn, just as you are able to show me, the outsider, Christianity. And for the very reason that you can do it, I cannot. Christianity has its soul in its externals; Judaism, on the outside, has only its hard protecting shell, and one can speak of its soul only from within. . . . You rightly put your finger on this difference in speaking of Moriah and Golgatha. But you have read your Genesis 22 badly. You have confused Abraham and Agamemnon. The latter indeed sacrificed what he had for the sake of something else that he wanted, or, if you like, that he considered it his duty to want. Indeed, he did not perform the sacrifice himself; he only gave it up, and stood with veiled head close by. But Abraham did not offer something, not "a" child, but his only son, and what is more, the son of the promise, and sacrificed him to the God of this promise (the traditional Jewish commentary reads this paradox into the text); the meaning of the promise according to human understanding becomes impossible through this sacrifice. Not for nothing is this story associated with our highest festivals; it is the prototype of the sacrifice not of one's own person (Golgatha), but of one's existence in one's people, of the "son" and of all future sons (for we base our claims before God on this sacrifice, or rather on this readiness to sacrifice, and it is the sacrifice of the father [not of the son], as is emphasized in the story). The son is given back; he is now only the son of the promise. Nothing else happens, no Ilium falls, only the promise remains firm; the father was ready to sacrifice not for the sake of some Ilium, but for the sake of nothing. Agamemnon sacrifices something "that he had"; Abraham, all that he could be; Christ, all that he is. Yes, that is really, as you say, "the whole difference." To the "naïve" laying claim to an inalienable right before God corresponds, you forget, just as naïve a taking up of a yoke of inalienable sufferings, which we—"naïvely"?—know is laid upon us (cf. the traditional commentary on Isaiah 53) "for the redemption of the world." (Lucifer? Please don't mix up those symbols!) . . . On the contrary: to the holy restlessness of your work corresponds in us a holy dread that the redemption might not come "before the time" (in which connection there are the most peculiar and grotesque legends, both old and new) ....[28]

In another letter:

Now to return to the subject: the two sacrifices, that on Moriah and that on Golgatha, have then this in common, as against all pagan sacrifices, that nothing was got out of them (since what was sacrificed is identical with what was given back), but the sacrifice itself becomes in effect the abiding object of faith, and thereby that which abides. That which abides is different; on the one hand an external community, and on the other an external man—and the consequences of this make mutual understanding so difficult that the one side is always being seduced into classifying the other with those that know of nothing abiding. Perhaps the readiest, if not also the most correct, antidote against this error of either side regarding the other as pagans is simply to reflect on our mutual possession of the Book. Your whole description of the Synagogue since A.D. 70 forgets, or refuses to recognize, that we consciously take upon ourselves "the yoke of the kingdom of heaven," that we pay the price for the sin of pride of non-cooperation, of walking without mediator in the light of God's countenance. We pay subjectively through suffering the consciousness of being shut out, of being alienated; and objectively, in that we are to you the ever-mindful memorial of your incompleteness (for you who live in a church triumphant need a mute servant who cries when you have partaken of God's bread and wine, "Master, remember the last things!").[29]

Jews may indeed be involved in the external life of the Christian world. But along with this external life

goes a pure inner Jewish life in all that serves the maintenance of the people, of its "life" insofar as it is not purchased from without, but must be worked out from within. Here belongs the inner Jewish task of ordering communal life, here Jewish theology, here the art

[28] See Letter No. 15.
[29] See Letter No. 15. An allusion to Herodotus' story of how Xerxes had a servant who stood behind him at table and said, "Master, remember the Athenians!" Rosenzweig is expressing the conviction which had led him into Judaism, that, in a Christianized civilization which had lost its eschatological sense, the Jews had the prophetic function of being a "peculiar people" living only for the "last things."

of the Synagogue (yes, its "beauty"!). These phenomena may comprise much that is strange—yet Judaism cannot but assimilate this strange element to itself; it acts like this of its own accord, even when it doesn't in the least want to do so. The prodigious strength of the tradition has this effect on us even when we are in fact unaware of it. The forms of the inner Jewish life are, however, quite distinct from all apparent parallels in civilizations. The art of the Synagogue does not enter into living relation with other art, nor Jewish theology with Christian theology, and so on; but Jewish art and theology, taken together, build up the Jews into a united whole, and maintain them in their form of life . . . . *Lasciava ogni cosa* [he gave up all things]—except for—*speranza* [hope]. Before the throne of God the Jew will only be asked one question: Hast thou hoped for the salvation? All further questions—the tradition doesn't say so, but I do—are addressed to you. Till then, Your, F.R.[30]

"My poor ben Judah!" Rosenstock replies. Have you not realized that the old European tradition, compounded as it was of Greeks and Romans, Jews and Christians, has now passed away? The operative distinctions now are nationalist, each people looking on itself somehow as a chosen people with a destiny to fulfill. Or, alternatively, we have the idea of a universalism in which we think of the rights of the human being as such.

You want to go not behind Europe and "my" Christianity, but behind "your" Jewish people, as it has mercilessly become, namely, ripe for rest and for the ending of its years of wandering. . . . God preserves his signs as long as our blindness needs them. But one must not rely on them as if they were eternal petrifications . . . .[31]

The old symbolic landmarks of European history are being removed. "The more one excavates Sumerians and Akkadians, the more completely and quickly will Europe forget Moriah, Marathon, Brutus; and, I add, it will be allowed to forget them. As little as Wilamowitz can rescue classical philology from death, can you rescue Hebrew in its metaphysical sense, especially if and just because it will once again become a language—that is, a national heritage planted in the soil of a people."[32]

[30] See Letter No. 15.
[31] See Letter No. 16.
[32] See Letter No. 16.

So Israel's time as the people of the Bible has gone by. Instead, we have Jewish nationalism in the form of Zionism. And Rosenzweig's Jewish ship knows very well where it is sailing.

Now you want to get on board and pilot yourself; then you will see—not know, but see, experience—that the ship is already sailing and is about to run aground, just as the ship of the Phaeacians was allowed to stand fast after it had finished the fated voyages of wandering Odysseus; and just as Odysseus at the end of his Greek wanderings went on pilgrimage to a people who knew nothing of seafaring in order to offer sacrifice and to pray, so the day of the eternal Jew beckons to its close.[33]

The "stubbornness of the Jews" is now no longer a Christian dogma. "Today, the task is to translate Christianity for the single isolated individual who can be anything: Jew, Christian, Pagan," the "moral proletariat" who did not exist in the old European tradition. And the operative background of the church, its real Old Testament, is now, in fact, its own church history; not the Old Testament of the people of Israel.

Rosenzweig agrees. Modern Christianity can fit the emancipated Jew into its thinking better than the Jew of Judaism. And, in Zionism, Judaism has produced a secularized form of the messianic movement. (Rosenzweig's criticism in these letters is directed at Zionism insofar as this represented a secular nationalistic substitute for the religious messianism of Judaism. Later in his life, I have been told, he came to see Zionism in a more favorable light. In any case he was not concerned to attack it as an attempt to work toward a political and temporal solution of the Jewish problem; and how great the need for a temporal solution was to become was not perhaps apparent to him in 1916.)

Nevertheless, in this new world of Christian universalism, perhaps Judaism is needed as "the one point of contraction," the reminder to Christianity of its original biblical roots. So long as this can happen, the old symbolic ordering of the European tradition will remain a power.

Sumerians and Akkadians will not neutralize Moriah, Marathon . . . but that somehow is the essence of revelation, to bring an absolute

[33] See Letter No. 16.

symbolic ordering to history . . . Jews, Greeks, and Romans will remain the everlasting contents of history because they are the Jews, Greeks, and Romans of Paul. . . . There must always be a demand for Greek . . . not from teachers of German and history, but from teachers of religion.[34]

This belief that it was the vocation of Judaism to remain "separated," pointing to the "last things" and to the One God beyond all our thinking and striving, was Rosenzweig's deepest conviction. Christianity, he believed, would go forward conquering the world, though largely at the cost of identifying its life with that of the world. It was perhaps easier to see Christianity in this way in 1916 than in 1945. Today Christianity also is being persecuted in many parts of the world, and we can nowhere speak with confidence of its triumphant progress toward the conquest of civilization.[35]

Rosenstock, however, seems to have had a prophetic inkling of what was to come and sensed that Rosenzweig's belief that the world was entering on a "Johannine age" of Christian civilization would not be realized. "If you would attribute to me," he wrote, "a *visio mundi naturaliter christiani* I am sensible that this expression stood, in its time, for something true. My strongest impression in the war is, however, precisely the turning, step by step, of the natural into the unnatural."[36]

Today, in 1945, Christians are more ready to appropriate their Jewish heritage and the eschatological elements in their own faith, whereas Jews are called not only to wait for the days of the Messiah but to draw on their resources of positive moral concern for the just ordering of the life of the community. So it might well be that today a new Rosenzweig and Rosenstock would find that they could not determine their standpoints in relation to each other in just the same way. But if this were so, it would only be true to the spirit of the letters. The dialogues

[34] See Letter No. 19.

[35] In my photograph reproduction of the figures of the church and the synagogue from the cathedral in Bamberg, the arm of the figure of the church, which should be carrying the scepter, is broken. Is this also symbolic?

[36] See Letter No. 10.

of the church and the synagogue must go on when and where such a relationship as that of Rosenzweig and Rosenstock arises. There is no final solution of these questions, valid for all contexts.

It is, indeed, in the perception that "speaking" must go on within an actual situation of relationship that our correspondents discover their common ground. Christianity and Judaism both speak of "Revelation"; and of Revelation coming not through generalized truths, but in the personal, concrete, and historic. "The Word of God" is not an expression of the general essence of Being but stands for the moment of communication. Rosenstock seems to have been feeling toward this in the thinking he had already done about the nature of language. Rosenzweig saw it as the conviction underlying the writing that he hoped to do.

I believe that there are in the life of each living thing moments, or perhaps only one moment, when it speaks the truth. It may well be, then, that we need say nothing at all *about* a living thing, but need do no more than watch for the moment when this living thing expresses itself. The dialogue which these monologues form between one another I consider to be the whole truth. That they make a dialogue with one another is the great secret of the world, the revealing and revealed secret, yes, the meaning of revelation.[37]

Today we find that, when Martin Buber writes on this theme in his *I and Thou*, he is welcomed by Christians as expressing a philosophy which is no less theirs than it is Jewish. [*N.B.*: See the "*Editor's Note*" immediately following Miss Emmet's essay, on p. 69.] But Rosenzweig had already sensed this as the point of "fundamental religious similarity" in the two faiths. Rosenstock was at first puzzled by this phrase. For, he says:

Over against the calm certainty of the Synagogue we have the perilous, adventurous character of our pattern of life ... [and] without this cultivation of the new man, Sunday is merely bourgeois, a mere Old Testament Sabbath for Christians .... But here breaks in abruptly that provoking forgiveness of sins, which produces the dramatic movement of the pattern. You can of course say that the Carpathian province of Siebenbürgen is equal to the Wallachian plain, but have you then achieved anything? In the same way, it is true that religion

[37] See Letter No. 17.

is religion, and remains so, and in this sense it is found among Jews and Christians. But put your hand on your heart (for we neither of us like them) and say whether it is not also found among Muslims.[38]

Rosenzweig replies: The two faiths are like images on two different coins, but behind, or rather in them, lies the same metal. Let us do as you say, and

just look for a moment at Islam ("hand on heart"). It is, for me, the crucial test. The "good Turk" has more in common with Goethe than with either Jew or Christian. . . . He doesn't know, and cannot know, the quite otherworldly attitude of the soul that yet breathes the world with every breath . . . . *How* that breathing of the world happens is the great contrast between Jew and Christian, but *that* it happens is their common ground. In Islam you will always find that God and the world always remain perfectly apart, and so either the divine disappears in the world or the world disappears in God. . . . Only for Jews and Christians exists that firm orientation of the world in space and time; the actual world and actual history exist; North, South, Past, Present exist, and are not "of God" . . . but they came of God, ought to become, and only therefore are. When Novalis says in his poem: "if I have only Thee," and when the Jew prays it— different names are addressed in poetry and adored in prayer, but to say "I" and "Thou" in this way, and to bind together "I" and "Thou" by "having"—this only Jew and Christian can do, and no one else.[39]

Rosenstock had asked one question more. His friend had hinted at dreams for work in higher Jewish religious education. Will he not explain them more explicitly? Or is it that "in order to live one's life one ought to keep silent about what one is and will be? Is there some αἰδώς, reticence, of the spirit, of which one can deprive oneself consciously and deliberately, but at the cost of losing real healthy activity?"[40] No, says Rosenzweig; that would be an evasion. The real reason he cannot yet speak of his future work is that he is not ready.

I have not yet the urge, and thus not yet the right, and because that is so, fortunately not yet either the maturity of technical scholarship .

[38] See Letter No. 18.
[39] See Letter No. 21.
[40] See Letter No. 20.

to work it out. . . . When the moment comes, one no longer speaks about αἰδώς.)[41]

Here the correspondence breaks off. When the moment did come, and the flame sprang to life, Rosenzweig's book, *The Star of Redemption*, poured out, posted in installments to Rosenstock and his wife, out of Macedonia, out of Serbia, out of hospitals and trains. This was told me in a personal letter from Rosenstock, and he adds: "His soul and his mind left his body behind and never fully took possession of it all again. His suffering from the atrophy of all his muscles and the writing of the *Star* in complete ecstasy—with no correction, in one white heat—were two aspects of one and the same process."

Rosenzweig had hoped for years of active work. But he brought back with him from the war the germs of a fatal disease (amyotrophic lateral sclerosis). Until his death in 1929, the paralysis of his bodily functions was steadily progressing. By a superhuman effort he was able to continue his work. When the power of speech failed, he worked on a specially constructed typewriter; later, his wife had to guess his meaning from hints and gestures as he pointed to the keyboard. In December, 1922 he began the translation and interpretation of the great Hebrew poet Yehudah ha-Levi. In May, 1924 he began, together with Martin Buber, a new German translation of the Bible. From his attic in Frankfurt-am-Main a stream of thought and inspiration poured into the world of his people.

Rosenstock (now Professor Rosenstock-Huessy of Norwich, Vermont) is, happily, still with us and able to speak to us on these matters as they confront us in our "post-Christian" age. For the debate continues.[*]

[41] See Letter No. 21.

[*] *Editor's note*—An aspect of the "debate" that may be of particular interest to many readers has to do with the "*I-Thou* philosophy" referred to in the essays of Professors Emmet and Altmann and in the footnote by the editor of *The Journal of Religion* to Miss Emmet's contribution (see especially p. 48). They are all quite correct in identifying *I-Thou* thinking with Eugen's and Franz' friend, Martin Buber, rather than with Eugen. Eugen's earliest "speech thinking" activities antedated Buber's (and Rosenzweig's) by a good many years, but in Eugen's judgment, the correct, truly

"existential" sequence is not *I-Thou* but *Thou-I*. In his view, Buber's *I-Thou* carries either the implication of a parity between the *I* and the *Thou*, or still worse, the implication that the *I* precedes the *Thou* in human experience. *Thou-I*, in contrast, quite accurately reflects an important reality that virtually everyone experiences, in one way or another—the fact that one is spoken *to*, one is nominated and addressed as a *Thou* (by one's parents, if no one else) *before* becoming an *I*. Cf. Eugen's essay "Liturgical Thinking," in the periodical *Orate Fratres* (January, 1950): "The soul must be called *Thou* before she can ever reply *I*, before she can ever speak of *us* and finally *it*. Through the four figures, *Thou*, *I*, *We*, *It*, the Word walks through us, the Word must call our name first . . ." (p. 12). This statement was far from being an afterthought in 1950. It was but the latest in a long series of published declarations to much the same effect, beginning before World War I and reflecting convictions held since 1902 or before. And Eugen's belief that *Thou* must, and does in fact, precede *I* in everyone's life experience was the burden of the fifth chapter of his *Angewandte Seelenkunde* (1924), echoing the *"Sprachbrief"* he had sent to Franz in 1916 (see note 212 on p. 170).

2

PROLOGUE/EPILOGUE TO THE LETTERS —FIFTY YEARS LATER

by Eugen Rosenstock-Huessy

Much nonsense has piled up about this "existential" correspondence. Some people speak of it as though it turned Eugen into a Jew, away from his Christian faith, and over the years some very foolish letters have been written to him on this account. And even now, years after his death, Franz is criticized by some for having "conceded" so much—too much!—to Christianity. Such interpretations, sometimes amounting to indictments, reflect serious misunderstanding on the part of those who offer them. Be that as it may, after fifty years it now should be possible for Eugen, as the surviving participant in the dialogue, to put the facts in somewhat better perspective than has been done hitherto, and to help the reader to focus on the actual happenings.

The real event of these letters, quite apart from the merits of what is said in them about Christianity and Judaism, is that the "objectivity" swindle of the academic class—"swindle" is perhaps too kind a word, since it implies that the culprits at least know what they are doing—was seen in its murderous impact on the Western World. A Jew and a Christian momentarily put aside their insoluble antithesis and united against self-styled "humanists" of all descriptions and dispensations. In their enmity towards the idols of relativism (in which not even Einstein believed), "objectivity" (largely spurious at best), abstract and nameless statistics (largely meaningless at best), the Jew and the Christian found a cause in common.

It was a drama in three acts. Those who read the letters alone are likely to go wrong, for there was a painful dialogue in 1913, preceding the letters by fully three years, and a robust epilogue in 1920. In the course of the three acts Franz and Eugen were existentially transformed. The reader may be put to some inconvenience by being asked to distinguish the three stages, but without his response or his willingness to share in this transformation he well may spare himself the bother of reading this volume.

ACT I – 1913

Franz, a mature scholar of twenty-seven, the author of a stupendous but as yet unpublished doctoral dissertation on *Hegel und der Staat* (Hegel and the State), goes to Leipzig, a great German university city, to study "some law." In this university, at the seat of the German Supreme Court, an uncle of Franz is a "Herr Geheimrat" in the Faculty of Law, and Eugen, at twenty-five the youngest "reader" in this same faculty, teaches courses in medieval constitutional history. Franz, a very superior mind, frequents courses and seminars conducted by this younger man.[1]

[1] *A digression on behalf of academic freedom*: In point of fact, Franz' going to Leipzig was prompted, in part at least, by a desire to do just this—to hear what a young, academically unorthodox *Privatdozent* had to say. The fact may startle some American readers, who will find it hard to imagine a tenureless instructor or assistant professor in an American institution ever being allowed to teach in a way that might attract post-doctoral students to his lectures. But the German *Privatdozent*, as the offspring of the Reformation, had a great deal more freedom to teach *his* "truth," in *his* way, than most academic people do in the United States, where universities are dominated by "administrators" and boards of trustees and even, in many cases, state legislatures, and where faculty and students have much less say than they should. In Germany before World War I, a young man who had established his academic credentials (by publishing a book or in some other way), and who had been admitted as *Privatdozent* in a university, could be pretty much his own man; in the slang of today, he was free "to do his own thing." Certainly there

On a summer evening in 1913, Franz, Eugen, and a son of the Herr Geheimrat, Rudolf Ehrenberg—he will shortly become a physiologist at the University of Göttingen—enter into a heated discussion of science and religion, inspired by a novel by Selma Lagerlöf, *The Miracles of the Antichrist*.

Eugen has not seen the novel since that night, and yet the last sentence of this book—on the miracle-working effigy of the Madonna in a Sicilian church—still reverberates in his mind. It reads, or it read in 1913: "Nobody can redeem men from their sufferings, but much shall be forgiven him who re-encourages them to bear these sufferings." This sentence is full of faith and full of scepticism, both, and on that warm evening its thesis was chased around and around—and around again. Franz, a student of philosophy and history for eight years by that time, defended the prevailing philosophical relativism of the day, whereas Eugen bore witness to prayer and worship as his prime guides to action. The three men separated very late that night, never to touch on the subject of religion again until 1916. In the interval, Franz and Eugen were to see each other only once, and on this occa-

---

was never any question of his being hired to fill a slot in a predetermined curriculum. In fact, he was not "hired" at all. Rather, he was authorized to teach under university auspices. *What* he taught was his own affair— and that of his students, since his income came *directly* from them (5 marks per student was the weekly fee). Accordingly, the *Privatdozent* had to be visibly competent and reasonably interesting in manner of presentation, and certainly he had to be "relevant," *in the judgment of his students*. Thanks in no small measure to the activities of *Privatdozenten*, German university curricula could and often did represent the particular interests, concerns, and needs of faculty on the one hand, and of students on the other, to a much greater extent than is usually the case in American institutions—except perhaps in some of the "underground" or "free" schools that have lately been organized on many American campuses, principally by students themselves on a spare-time (and of course non-credit) basis. Stigmatizing such underground activities as the nefarious doings of "Communist anarchists," "extremists," etc. is folly. The real scandal in American higher education is not the rebellion of students against the academic establishment, but the stultifying "objectivity" and "neutrality" of the academic establishment itself—"neutrality" that is conveniently forgotten by far too many administrators and faculty members when they see a chance of getting big money from the military establishment or from what is euphemistically called "the business community."

sion (July 30, 1914) the outbreak of World War I prevented any religious dialogue. (The meeting, very brief, took place in the home of Eugen's parents in Berlin. Eugen, his mind occupied by the prospect of going into the army on August 2, used the occasion of Franz' visit to dictate—standing under a cold shower—some sort of "urgent memorandum" for the foreign office. Franz promised to deliver the memorandum.)

For quite some time, then, Eugen remained unaware of the significant events that had ensued in the wake of the dialogue of 1913. As he was to learn later, his outburst in the Lagerlöf debate had shaken Franz' agnosticism to the extent that in the months from June to September, 1913 Franz was resolved to become a Christian, and to confess as radically as Eugen had to a faith in the revealed, living God. But in September, 1913 Franz attended services of the highest Jewish holidays, and his participation in this act of divine worship convinced him, much to his own surprise, that he could remain, that he would *have to remain*, a Jew—but on a different basis than before. He was, in effect, converted to Judaism as the guiding force in his life. But Eugen, and the point is worth repeating, knew nothing of the intense resolve to which his confession of faith in the Leipzig conversation had given rise, nor of its later modification by Franz' visit to the Jewish place of worship.

Act II — 1916

Eugen returns from the Verdun front to his garrison, for a few weeks. The other partner of 1913, Rudolf Ehrenberg, visiting Eugen and his wife, Margrit, tells them of Franz' conversion to Judaism and of the following years in Franz' life, and urges Eugen to write to Franz, who by this time is serving on the Macedonian front as a noncommissioned officer in the German army. Hence Eugen's letter of May 29, unwittingly initiating his and Franz' dialogue on Judaism and Christianity.

Since the common basis that was established in 1913 is an unusual one, it deserves further definition. Franz and Eugen came to agree on the ultimate futility of the shilly-shallying academic shibboleths of their day—objectivity, humanism, and the so-called enlightenment. They agreed that real people can be Jews or Christians, but they may not play the roles "Benjamin Franklin" or "Thomas Paine," at least not for long, since there can be no common sense—certainly no *good* sense shared in common—among men who are content to be ciphers dealing in generalities and platitudes. Behind this point of agreement against all positivists and pragmatists neither Franz nor Eugen would retreat, and in this determination they now owned a united front for Jews and Christians. This Eugen's stubbornness had imposed in 1913, but he certainly never expected his friend to emerge, within this common front, as a devoted (not merely "devout") Jew. How Franz defended his new position makes the contents of these letters, but in them, the pendulum swings from faith in the Christian revelation to a faith in Moses and the Prophets, and both faiths have their day in court.

ACT III — 1920

The dualism of Eugen, a professing Christian, and Franz, now a confessing Jew, is again put to the test—this time as part of a tripartite situation. A third man (Rudolf Hallo), under the influence of Eugen, has toyed with the idea of baptism for himself, but with Franz' help—he boldly appointed him as second in command (and heir) in the Jewish Lehrhaus—this youngster re-establishes his Jewish identity. But now he plagues Franz with outbursts of his too violent, even fanatical, return to the Jewish fold, and Franz has to put his foot down, insisting that the community of all those who confess, against those who merely think timelessly, embraces *all* believers: "*Sprache ist doch mehr als Blut.*" (Speech is more than blood.)[2]

Confronted by the excessive zeal of his reconverted Jewish friend, Franz declared: "The walls have fallen. Where we met, where Eugen and I met, no antiquated walls separate man and man . . . 'For those who have awakened the cosmos has become a community' [Herakleitos]. Our communion—which I tried to resist between 1913 and 1917—is safe. Judaism, Christianity,

[2] Franz Rosenzweig, *Briefe* (Berlin: Schocken Verlag, 1935), Nr. 339, October 6, 1929.

Creation: what has happened to us with regard to all three is the living faith, and no [mere] orthodoxy can chain this stream of life, which must achieve our resurrection from the cemeteries of Germany and of Europe. How the shape of this resurrection may *look*, is no proper cause for worry. We have to *live* it" [emphasis supplied].[3]

And to Eugen's wife Margrit, Franz wrote on June 15, 1920, in a letter hitherto unprinted: "It is a great act of mercy that God once has uprooted me out of life during my life. From July to September, 1913 I was quite willing to die—to let everything within myself die. But this may not be made into a rule. Most men simply live their life's fate, or destiny, and nothing more. It is the extraordinary in us that God, in our case, has not only spoken to us through our lives; in addition he has made the life around us fall down like the wings of a theatrical decoration, and on the empty stage he has spoken to us. We have to know that this is something peculiar, and we must construe no hard and fast rule from it."[4]

[3] *Briefe*, pp. 381 ff.
[4] From an unpublished letter.

3

THE DIALOGUE
ON CHRISTIANITY AND JUDAISM*

1   *Eugen to Franz*

May 29, 1916

My gallant Unteroffizier[1] Rosenzweig,

While I am greatly enjoying taking your place here,[2] and staying on for as long as I can, leaving no room for you, the time seems to have become ripe for a correspondence between us. If it has not been quite appropriate so far, we can now at least play a game in the open. Having read your article on Schelling,

---

* These letters were translated into English by Dorothy M. Emmet, from the appendix in Franz' *Briefe* (Berlin: Schocken Verlag, 1935), during World War II, and the version printed here is essentially hers, though a number of editorial revisions have been made, and footnotes have been added, with a view to making the correspondence somewhat more readily accessible to American readers. Further, beginning with Letter 17, the order of the letters differs from that in the 1935 printing and in Dr. Emmet's original translation. Heartfelt thanks are extended Franz' widow (now Mrs. Edith Scheinmann), for permission to include English translations of his letters in this volume, and Miss Emmet, for permission to make use of her sympathetic translation of the correspondence.

[1] Noncommissioned officer.

[2] That is, at the Rosenzweig home, at Terrasse 1, Kassel, where this letter was written.

I feel for the first time without any reservations that I am at one with you in scholarly research. Of course, there is still the question of whether you are at one with me, or will be when I throw away my professional mask and appear before you in the part of a philosopher. To be jurist and historian has been burdensome to me for a long time. Now that I am boldly philosophizing in my work, and not only in the privacy of my thoughts, I must write to you in this capacity too.

Your paper,[3] a masterpiece of explication, has stirred me more than you will think necessary. But—it is all completely in the present to me. I have you to thank for an illumination of the Revolution of 1789–1800 in psychological—stupid word!, it means, in plain German, *visual*—form and interpretation: and that at a time when I believe I have at last just taken the saving step into a system. To be sure, it is not at all from merely historical interest, and not as a member of a school, but in the fashion of 1916—not as a disciple of one of my colleagues of 1800, but as one nonetheless soaked in the ideas of Schelling, Hegel, Fichte.

Since I am at this very moment sitting in your own house, in the mood of exaltation that you draw from the faded page, I must take the risk—without νεμεσᾶν[4]—of divulging to you this constellation of stars—*doctor haruspici*.[5] So, Master Examiner of Entrails, I am certainly not yet delivering myself up at your table of guinea pigs and rabbits, but I warn you: the dragon's seed is springing up in your own house.

I philosophize in the form of a calendar (cf. Rudi's[6] style of

---

[3] "The Oldest Program of a System for German Idealism" (*Das älteste Systemprogramm des deutschen Idealismus*), composed by Schelling but preserved in Hegel's handwriting, had been discovered and edited by Franz, but had not yet been published. It finally appeared in 1917, under the auspices of the Heidelberger Akademie der Wissenschaften, and was later included in Franz' *Kleinere Schriften* (Berlin: Schocken Verlag, 1937).

[4] Calling down a nemesis.

[5] Examiner of entrails; omen-taker.

[6] Dr. Rudolf Ehrenberg, a cousin of Franz, was (and is) a brilliant physiologist, whose *Theoretische Biologie* (1923) was, as Franz was later to put it, "the first work to subordinate the doctrine of organic nature to

preaching); and science, which I loved so much from a distance, is at last taken captive and bound and brought along on the chariot wheel of theology. Apart from the calendar—that is, the rhythm of time (for mere Time is nothing, and only becomes something through the "recurrence of the same")[7]—my thoughts are haunted by a struggle against dialectic and the tabulating of conclusions: Major Premise, Minor Premise, Conclusion, i.e. against the *three*. I am all for the *four*, two squared as the foundation of all comparison, relation, and relativity. These two are the formal principles that determine the structure of the whole; the structure itself, however . . . .

Well, it is queer enough to pass on to you even as much as I have by field post to Valandowo.[8] Today, I only want to make a practical proposal. I am not at all fond, generally, of any of the novelties that are produced by war, and therefore I fully appreciate your decision not to print the Program before Janua Reclusa.[9] But that was before I left and now, more than ever, I should like to make an earnest appeal to you: everything is ready here, down to the dot on the last i. This is a book only for the people who had already suffered from philosophy before 1914. To the intellectual recruits who will come back from the war it means nothing and will never mean anything; it's Hecuba to these *homines inhumanissimi et novi.*[10] But for people of the older generation, like myself, you are providing a refined pleasure, just during this time of preparation, when you illuminate and close our "neo-romanticism" as in a focus. Let two hundred copies be taken off in proof, or even as a small first edition, and distribute them—for people have gotten out of the habit of buying books in this time of "war literature." At the conclusion of peace, when the initiate express their delight at the treat you have

---

the law of real, irreversible time" (quoted in N. N. Glatzer, *Franz Rosenzweig: His Life and Thought* [New York: Schocken Books, Inc., 1953], p. 200). His other writings, most recently *Metabiologie* (1950), are also of very great importance.

[7] A phrase in Nietzsche's *Thus Spoke Zarathustra.*

[8] In Macedonia, where Franz was stationed at the time.

[9] That is, before the return of peace, as symbolized by the shutting of the gates of the temple of Janus.

[10] Men of few years and less humanity.

given them, it will be possible to arrange for a larger second edition. Don't be afraid of the smallness of the enterprise. You sit so perfectly—I don't want to say in the heart of philosophy, because you and philosophy have no heart—but indeed ἐν φρεσί [11]—as the myth of these matters and questions has it—that your abundant and full knowledge becomes apparent even to the blindest eyes. So there is no reason for you to fear that people may make a mistake about your stature. Once more, I say: *publish!* I will gladly read the proofs. You yourself will be glad to have this behind you when, once again as a free man, you don't exactly sing, but——. Incidentally, I should like to mention that by so doing you would safeguard against Braun[12] your not only delightfully done, but also most fascinating, exposition of the discovery. Otherwise, perhaps, a mere "publication" of it must be reckoned with. . . .

So—please don't respond after the fashion of an antiballoon battery,[13] but consider the matter seriously.

Your Eugen Rosenstock

2 Franz to Eugen

Dear R.,

I fully anticipated your letter, so much so that I could almost have answered the second part several weeks ago. I too have indulged for some considerable time the thought of how nice it would be to have gotten both books out of the way, the thin one and the fat one, by the end of the war; and especially in the case of the thin one, I was highly intrigued by the fact, of which I am well aware, that it is really finished. As for the susceptibility

---

[11] The Homeric term for the seat of the passions and affections, i.e. the "midriff."

[12] Dr. Otto Braun (d. 1922), a professor of philosophy and a "Schelling expert" who could be expected to take a proprietary interest in Franz' discovery—if he got wind of it prior to Franz' publication of the text.

[13] "BAK," i.e. *Ballonabwehrkanonen.*

of the public, that seems to me almost perfectly restored; the war has lasted such a long time that a new kind of life has quite naturally developed at home . . . .

Now before the war, I had thought the matter out like this: I should go to Meiner with the sensational little essay, he should take that from me and afterwards be the more ready to take the fat Hegel[14] also—as something that had to appear soon afterwards and, after the sure success of the small publication, as something that would no longer have to bear the stigma (well-deserved, by the way) of its being the work of a "beginner."

A refined plan of attack on the thousand-headed monster—but now, when it seems that the war may last an incalculable time longer, I am less set in these old plans. If it were possible, I would prefer to get *everything* published and out of the way now, simply so as not to have to pick up in 1918 where I left off in 1914. The Hegel won't do now—in the first place because the manuscript itself would still cost me about two months work, working my hardest (the archives at Stuttgart, and all kinds of literature), and I would also have to be in Berlin to correct proofs.

But the Schelling essay will do. The notes that are lacking could be dispensed with, and the only thing that would still need work is the second section, in which the text must be printed. For this reproduction of the text must be "diplomatic" to the point of being unreadable (with new paragraph marks, etc.). Only afterwards, when it is served up to the reader bit by bit in my own sauce (and then even the spelling will have to be modernized, not to mention the punctuation) will he be able to get a comfortable impression of the text. You could easily see to that during a casual stay in Berlin, and also ask permission to publish the "Hegel manuscript,"[15] a point over which it is quite possible that Georg Lasson might still put a spoke in our wheel (also

[14] *Hegel und der Staat*, largely completed in 1912, but not published (and then with certain revisions) until 1920.

[15] That is, Schelling's *"Systemprogramm"* (see note 3). Dr. Georg Lasson (1862–1932), referred to later in the sentence, was the famous Hegel scholar who edited the 18-volume Leipzig edition of Hegel's collected works, and the Hegel Archive (after 1907).

Meiner would first of all say that it could appear as a publication of the Hegel Archive. As a matter of fact, I am horrified at the idea of publishing privately, and of distributing it as well. If Meiner accepted it for publication, I would consider that much more dignified than the Bohemian style of publishing over my own name;[16] if he put it in a small format, because of the present paper shortage, then so much the better. Why must learned books, nowadays, look like "Königshaus und Stämme"[17] instead of like Haym's *Hegel*? (The text of my Hegel is no more voluminous than Haym's, but what a ponderous tome mine could become if published according to present-day fashion, instead of in the manner of the attractive pocket editions of 1857.[18])

The Schelling essay fails in its contents to take note of the latest Hölderlin publications (in the second impression of Böhme's edition, and somewhere else as well).

Now, down to business: You have never—I mean to say during the last few years—been to me anything other than a "philosopher"; I have always felt that the jurist and the historian were only incidental tendencies. The jurist and historian would have been at the best interesting to me; the would-be philosopher has become a corner of my life. That the *Privatdozent* and the lieutenant has (or should I say "have"?) not noticed this, I put down to my churlish behavior. I have not the least reason to be grateful to you for the part you play in my life; it is your barest duty and obligation to be just what you are. The aforementioned churlishness now expresses itself again and says that it can't make out much of anything from the hints of your philosophy that you have written down—and instead of hints it demands a sample! I have plenty of time here, and you need only keep to the weight limit. (Just one note: do you know the number Four within Hegel's dialectic? You will find the scattered passages best in the tables of contents wherever he makes four divisions.

---

[16] *Selbstverlags.*

[17] That is, like Eugen's book, *Königshaus und Stämme in Deutschland Zwischen 911 und 1250*, first published in 1914, and reprinted in 1965 by Scientia Verlag.

[18] And, true enough, it was as a "ponderous" volume that *Hegel und der Staat* was printed in 1920!

Four appears particularly in the Philosophy of Nature; it is the *nunc stans* there.) So, since I have altogether taken you to be a philosopher, your transition to a written system isn't so important to me. You were a philosopher already, and will never be one in the sense in which you now intend it. There are no longer any "colleagues" of the men of 1800—and there ought not to be. Hegel spoke the truth when he (implicitly) said what he (explicitly) knew: that he was the end of philosophy. (Incidentally, where could you look for truth in the world if the self-consciousness lied?) The problem posed through the act of Thales, of "philosophy in itself," was settled then, and the man who was chained to this problem, the philosopher, has become superfluous (a "professor"). From then on there are only "doctors," as they call themselves. I would not go beyond these hints were it only so as not to disturb your pleasant combination of *doctor haruspici*. But otherwise you had better call me *augur auguri*,[19] since this title of Doctor, which you mean and claim, can only be bestowed by posterity and be borne where the dumb and friendly lions steal around.[20] The works of a *haruspex*[21] are *opera posthuma*[22]—thus I want to get rid of them (Sir, they stink already!).

The charge of heartlessness, which you level at me and at philosophy, I put down to the account of your recent marriage, from the heights of which you look proudly on the confused crowd of bachelors, far below you; hence, I congratulate only your wife "from my heart," since for you I am only ἐν φρεσί[23] and remain your,

Franz Rosenzweig

The more than "civil," in fact even human, style of address[24] on

[19] One soothsayer to the other.
[20] An allusion to the House of Hades in Gluck's *Orfeo ed Euridice* or some similar opera.
[21] Examiner of entrails.
[22] Works performed on dead organisms.
[23] Midriff.
[24] The letter was addressed to: "Herrn Eugen Rosenstock, M. Br. Herrn Kommerzienrat Rosenzweig. Kassel. Terrasse 1"—that is, to Mr. Eugen Rosenstock, at the home of Franz' parents.

this letter will satisfy your request not to have the answer of "an antiballoon battery" (I couldn't very well call you "Doctor" immediately after what we have just said, and *"Privatdozent"* would be brutal).

3   *Eugen to Franz*

Kassel, June 30, 1916

Dear Franz . . .

Rudi was there, and that was fine. He played the part of devil's advocate—that is to say, your advocate—almost as though he were already a student of your Jewish theology. I have sent you König,[25] not with any idea of your being interested in it already, but rather in order to arouse such an interest. Also, I rather think that it is the misfortune of the Jews that they—"don't want to hear the Truth."[26] I too dissuade you from Meiner, without feeling too happy about Diederichs.[27] I don't intend for a moment to send you anything that isn't ready for the press. One sends to one's antithesis, if possible, only *après la lettre.*[28] I am sorry enough that only today I had to pass on to Pope Stutz *avant la lettre* an article that I had sweated over for the *Savigny Zeitschrift.*[29] I am at present specialist in popular and country calendars and Freemasonry. Why don't you become a Jachin Tem-

[25] Dr. Eduard König, a professor of Old Testament at Bonn, had recently published a short book on *Der ewige Jude* (The Wandering Jew).

[26] In 1849, the Frankfurt parliament asked the king of Prussia to become emperor. He refused to do so, whereupon the deputy Johann Jacoby exclaimed: "It is the misfortune of kings that they do not want to hear the truth."

[27] Eugen Diederichs, a publisher of books and of the magazine, *Die Tat,* which is referred to in Franz' letter of July 6.

[28] In the jargon of engraving, *avant la lettre* is a print taken as a first rough proof, *après la lettre* is a print taken when the engraving is in a finished state.

[29] Germany's leading magazine of legal history, *Zeitschrift der Savignystiftung für Rechtsgeschichte,* of which Ulrich ("Pope") Stutz was the tyrannical editor. The article referred to was: "Die Verdeutschung des Sachsenspiegels," vol. 37 (1916), pp. 498–504.

pli?[30] Incidentally, if one of your friends were no longer an important person but simply ill, what would you do with him? That's where the real crux comes for your

Rosenstock

4 *Franz to Eugen*

July 6, 1916

Dear R.,

I have given you no information because, except for the form from the Königlichen Bibliothek[31] and a reader's ticket with some remarks from you on it, I knew of nothing further. Perhaps a letter from you has gone astray. Or perhaps not? Today your card of the 30th came. I leave everything to you. I don't put any value on the addition of a facsimile. I can't establish the text of the diplomatic reproduction myself, even through a copy, because I have nothing to go on. With my crude self-taught philology I should only have learnt how to do it in this flagrant example—like everything in philology. But if the publisher himself wants a facsimile, that would be quite all right. I don't know anyone besides Diederichs. Naturally, I am not happy with him either: he is a caricature, and not a natural man, but all the same a good fellow (*Die Tat* is now actually a good journal).

As a student of Freemasonry, you must have a look at Horneffer's *Unsichtbaren Tempel*.[32] I know it badly, or rather not at all *a posteriori*, but *a priori* it interests me greatly, and I have already made use of it several times, without really meaning to do so, as illustrating a negative starting point—evil as appearance. I don't know whether I ought to concern myself with it positively, but the fact that you know it shows me how pointless this exchange of postcards between us is (or would be). And whether, or in what sense, we are antitheses (that is, today), I simply don't know; when we talked to each other in Berlin, at Easter

---

[30] In Freemasonry, a term signifying a pillar in the Temple of Solomon. Neither of the correspondents was a Mason.

[31] Royal Library.

[32] August Horneffer's Invisible Temple.

1914, it was not yet possible for me to recognize myself even as an antithesis in much of what you were saying; your Italian ideas were then so strange to me.[33] Of course, we were thesis and antithesis in Leipzig (but not on a level, because I was your pupil). What we are now, *I don't know*, be it only because I don't know myself definitely as an –ologist or an –osopher. On the whole, I now know less than I did before; I am waiting.

But König? I have not been able to get anywhere with him, either as –ologist or as –osopher, or as "man who knows," or as "man who waits." It is simply and absolutely nothing. (I have just read something quite meaningless by him, *Das antisemitische Hauptdogma*.)[34]

To explain myself to you more clearly: I used to have a whole series of books and articles, "ready, as it were, in my head"—and not merely in my head—but incidentally very fine books, all things such as one wishes he could write. At present, I am not making any further plans for them (perhaps they will implicitly come to light again some day, in the course of my life, but I am not planning *anything* any longer). When the war is over and the Hegel is in print, I shall not be ready with a plan for some further book. You must have noticed in the Hegel that its real reason for being was not an interest in Hegel, but my wish to make *a book*. (Just as you always used to say, I wrote too "finely": that is what I mean.) My whole past development from my early years, from when I was a boy in the middle school (to quote you,[35] but it is true, every word of it), has been determined by this urge after "productivity for its own sake." There is only one person who knows me in this connection, right through in all phases: Trudchen Oppenheim[36] in Kassel—and no one else. But that is now a matter of the past. I have changed from a man who wanted to do nothing but produce, into one who has no plan, but only problems, without knowing or even caring whether anything ever comes of it. Now I "ask," whereas formerly I

[33] From August 1, 1913 through March 31, 1914 Eugen had been occupied with research in central Italy.

[34] The Main Dogma of Anti-Semitism.

[35] In the preface to *Königshaus und Stämme*, Eugen had written of his "Days in High School."

[36] Franz' cousin and confidant, Gertrud Oppenheim (née Frank).

"shaped" (always taking the will for the deed, as indeed one must).

So I am no longer an antithesis to you. Where there is any antithesis, you ought not to throw it at my head, out of complete ignorance, in pointed messages on postcards. Whether you write to me *avant la lettre* or not, my present relationship to you is a relationship *avant la lettre*, and if you confide it to me (as you have every right to do, and with my complete approval), that does not prevent me from holding a conversation *avant la lettre* with your ghost, which finds itself in Macedonia at the moment. The reason is that for me, generally speaking, there is now in fact only *avant la lettre* in the world, whereas before, everything, even the "present," was to me *après la lettre* (another way of putting what we already said higher up).

"I have spoken, howgh!" And if you write any more nonsense to me about it, someone will be really angry with you, namely your,

F. Rosenzweig

5   *Eugen to Franz*

Kassel, July 12, 1916

Dear Franz,

You shall hear from me again as soon as I can manage it from the front, but today, during my visit to say goodbye to your parents, I just want to ask you the humble question, whether or not you consider Mohr-Siebeck suitable; I certainly do, particularly on account of the size of the books that Mohr usually goes in for. Isn't the photograph of the text charming?[37] It is the first one larger than life size that I know.

Your E. R.

6   *Eugen to Franz*

July 19, 1916

Dear Franz,

You mustn't—or to be exact, you can no longer—expect a

[37] That is, of the Schelling find.

proper or even a simple answer to your letters to me. From Kassel I could still talk to you in and from the setting of a personal relationship, by relating conversation and news of your parents' house. Just as your letter had particularly whetted my appetite, the delicate hand of war came and tore me from the life of scholar and teacher, and then from my married life—which is, as you accuse it of being, a happy one. In consequence, I have a week's complete vacation. I am once again at large and far away from you. Our paths seem to have diverged far from each other. I am looking for what you have finished with; what you are looking for, I had in the beginning. *In principio erat verbum*,[38] and for so long there was confusion. And when the Word becomes flesh, it also becomes light from above. In comparison, Goethe's froglike view: in the beginning was the Act, is quite devoid of any stars; that is to say, it is a soulless system, possessing mass and weight and yet also terribly actual and objective. But you know all that just as well as I do. Right now I am so firmly mounted on the dualism of Above and Below, of Yonder and Here as it is untruly called, that I must either keep quiet or else talk with you from this position in the saddle. I have sent you the two writings by König,[39] though their execution is flabby and weak, because the view presented in them is right and apt. You see, this man shows me, just because his own intellectual gifts are indifferent, the value of the *position* that he holds. Couldn't you, without difficulty, now write the same thing yourself, on *your* level, with the help of his efforts? For who still takes Israel and the eternal Jew seriously? I can only see—you and König! Though I frankly acknowledge that I myself make yet a third. The whole decomposing, short-winded Zionist movement blows itself to pieces, as it were, before this enduring idea of the "eternal" (God *and* the Jews)—not to speak of the other wing, that of the stern, "Love the remotest as yourself" of Herr Cohen.[40]

[38] In the beginning was the word.

[39] Eugen can't definitely recall the title of the second work referred to, but it may have been König's *Geschichte der alttestamtlichen Religion* (1910).

[40] For Hermann Cohen's influence on Franz, see Alexander Altmann's essay.

Just now I am reading Cohen's freer master, Kant, whose translation of philosophy into German (I mean intellectually) has captured me once again, as has his despairing clutch at freedom of thought outgrowing language. You know that I had read Schelling before, and then Hegel. I am not sending you anything, not so much because I don't want to, as because it won't serve, owing to the character of the thing as a whole. Or—can you make *anything* out of the following outline??[41]

1. The Year

2. Course of the Year	4. The World's Year
3. Year in one's life	5. The Church's Year

1. The Year

2 December: Napoleon's Day: Foundation. Those who take part in the war in 1916 come together in order to conjure up the present.

Gathering	1 January:	New Year: Rebirth
	6 January:	Epiphany: Freedom
	18 January:	Versailles: Language
	28 January:	Charlemagne: Epoch of the World
Splitting up	15 February:	Lessing: Departure of the new knighthood
	24 February:	Leap Day: Watch
Experience	11 March:	Carnival night
	15 March:	Caesar: Despotic Power
	21 March:	First day of Spring: Compulsion
Knowledge	8 April:	Humboldt: Completeness
	21 April:	Luther in Worms: Facts
	24 April:	Kant: Doubt
	30 April:	Gauss: Numerical Relationship
Wealth	2 May:	Gorlice: Order
	5 May:	Marx: Unity
	18 May:	St. Paul's Church: Equality
	21 May:	Dürer: Abundance

[41] This draft was more than a year old when this letter was written.

Decision	1 June:	Accident
		Necessity
		Loyalty $\left.\right\}$ Analysis
		Justice
		Discipline
Connection	4 July:	1776: Shame
	9 July:	Zeppelin: Progress
	15 July:	Eclipse of the Moon: Nature
	30 July:	Death of Bismarck: Death
Will	2 August:	Home
	7 August:	Luttich: War
	17 August:	Frederick the Great: Fate
	28 August:	Goethe: Impulse to create
Imagination	2 September:	Map of Peoples of the World
	10 September:	Helmholtz: Science
	20 September:	1870: Freemasonry, World Citizenship
	25 September:	1555: World View
People	2 October:	Rembrandt: Art
	7 October:	Day of Atonement: Blood relationship
	12 October:	1492: *Elective Affinities*
	18 October:	1830: Monarchy
	18 October:	1813: Imperial Power
Church	1 November:	All Saints' Day: Confession
	2 November:	All Souls' Day: Parable
	4 November:	Luther: Translation
	10 November:	Schiller: Truth
	17 November:	Monasticism
	28 November:	Bull *Unam sanctam* 1302: the Church
Individual	2 December:	Disintegration
	2 December:	Mozart: Beauty
	3 December:	First Sunday in Advent: Prayer
	10 December:	Second Sunday in Advent: Scripture
	17 December:	Third Sunday in Advent: Community
	24 December:	Fourth Sunday in Advent: Christianity
	25 December:	Love

This "Calendar of the Year"[42] is being worked out. Whether it will, or even can be, developed fully is hard to say. Unfortunately, my physical strength is also much reduced, and that makes a considerable difference just when there are other obstacles in addition, such as military service, etc. For you know that, except when I am in a state of trance, I only write in a dry and stumbling way. You will, meantime, have received your *Ethics*. It had still to be sent to me from Kassel. I will, then, "transcribe" the text as soon as possible, though a skillful compositor could read Hegel at least as well as he could read my pen. Meanwhile, you may have made up your mind with regard to the publisher, and recommended yourself dutifully to Mohr or Reimer.

Please don't let yourself be deterred from answering again by this abortive *nihil*, and thus we may at last get into marching step. Today I only want to end with the assurance that I do care about it.

Your Eugen Rosenstock

7   *Franz to Eugen*

September 5, 1916

Dear R.,

All right. That *will do*. Even if it *need* not be done. But that, generally speaking, is the law under which all our thinking has stood, *post Hegel mortuum*, that this great, serious "Now this, now this, now that, must be done," this mighty objective *neutrum*, no longer exists, and now in its place only "*I* must" is valid, and only insofar as the "I" is, after all, a fragment of the "It," does this "I must" become something it did not intend to be at all, namely: "It must." The ἄνθρωπος θεωρητικός,[43] that greatest and most enduring achievement of the Greeks, enduring because it remained without antithesis in itself (even the "Ideas" themselves already found their negation in antiquity itself)—this "the-

---

[42] "*Jahrgang.*"
[43] The conceptualizing human being.

91

oretic man" has now at last *cessé de regner*. The νοῦς πρακτικός[44] now has to do everything, even think; the νοῦς θεωρητικός[45] is no longer part of the human soul.

I had written as far as this on the day that your letter of July 19 arrived, and so had the good intention of answering it at once. Now it has remained on one side, and I want to see how I can get into it again. But I'll have to start afresh.

The "calendar form" is the method of this kind of philosophy. So the pure calendar ("course of the year") occupies the place in the system where the Idealists put logic (The Critique of Pure Reason, *Wissenschaftslehre*,[46] Transcendental Idealism). In order to establish at once my claim to have understood you: The course of the year = Nature; the year in one's life = ethics; the world's year = philosophy of history; the church's year = . . . and so incidentally in the further series we have the usual Idealist system. More exactly, the course of the year is not merely logic, but what Hegel originally meant by phenomenology: the method presented in all its aspects *in statu nascendi*[47] from what is experienced. Now for a moment, in order to clarify (and only for this purpose), here is a contrary scheme: You philosophize in the form of Time, so I want for a moment to philosophize in the form of Space.

1. The scene (Kassel, Wilhelmshöhe, Vierwaldstätter See, Homer's Sun, Cornwall—Island—Brittany, Harz—Frankfurt—Weimar, Göttingen, Munich, Freiburg).
2. The Universe
3. The Houses (parents' house, school house, barracks, strange houses, one's own house, the town hall)
4. The World
5. The Cathedral

Why does that do too? Obviously because everything that is essentially an ingredient of the end can also be beginning and middle (way, method). Because God has created the world, one can philosophize in the form of Space or of Time (and naturally

[44] The poetical mind.
[45] The conceptualizing mind.
[46] The name given to Fichte's philosophical system.
[47] In the condition or state of being born.

Time is of more use than Space, because Space is indeed only a sensible appearance of Time, as my alternative scheme very nicely shows—historical geography is nothing but a joke tacked on to world history, and so forth). So then, one can philosophize in the form of the *World*. Idealism, however, did not do so. Instead, it philosophized in the form of the *soul*.

Up to now we have looked on this as if it were a necessity. But that we did so means that we accepted without question the Idealist presupposition, which in the last resort is simply that philosophy is necessary for the sake of knowledge. If this presupposition is now abandoned—I notice to my satisfaction that I am taking up again the threads that I started to spin on the first page of this letter—if it is abandoned, then in the place of the single method of the one "truth," there open up the many methods of infinite life (the former method was in fact Idealism, the history of which is the whole "history of philosophy," since the way Thales presented the problem in the beginning was not merely philosophy, but already, in effect, Idealism). Hegel's Phenomenology (despite everything, a phenomenology of *Logic*) was a premature attempt, and in the first part of the system, and then in fact dropped. On the other hand, phenomenologies have now, quite seriously, to be the first part of future systems, and, as it were, their author's credentials and authorization. In the Calendar method (because of the "transcendental" character of Time) there still remains the fiction, or rather the claim, to be more than a view of the world coordinated with a view of one's life. But I should like to show you a crude example that will also "do." Listen! I am a painter:

1. Impressions (my "inwardly full of form").
2. Nature ("most certainly art is contained in nature . . .").
3. Technique (the "problem of form"—"most certainly art is contained in nature; *whoever can pull it out, possesses it!*").
4. Object ("The eye is man's *noblest sense*").
5. Work (conversation with Melanchthon concerning the simplifying style).

You cannot say that all this has its place somewhere in the *universal* system of the world, since that is only true of Parts 2–5. But the soul of the system, Part 1, can be worked out only by the painter himself, and the extent to which Part 1 is decisive for

Parts 2–5 you yourself know and feel better than I could tell you.

Just *because* Part 1 is absolutely personal, and because this personal character must not (as Hegel still believed in the Phenomenology) be overcome in order that the system may follow it, but because it is being purified step by step in the system, the system seen from the point of view of the author is the way to salvation.

We will leave König alone. I don't find even the modest merits that you claim for him. About Cohen, you ought not to write (to me) as you did (and as I well understand); I know him personally, and reverence him infinitely on the grounds of that personal knowledge, not on the basis of his published works. That is my private affair, but just for that reason . . . .

There is still room on the paper, but there is a noise going on overhead and this letter must go at last. Siebeck[48] will have sent the Schelling essay to my old friend Mehlis[49] for his judgment—an amusing thought!

With warm greetings from your F. Rosenzweig

I have just noticed that this whole page is blank. I can't cope with these envelopes, which is another reason why the war must come to an end sometime.

A request: I would like to read texts of the Fathers of the Church and the Scholastics, but I don't know the existing editions (with the exception of Lietzmann's, which I have almost eaten up), and you of course have them all at your fingertips. Please write to my parents, or directly to Kay: he ought to let me have the catalogues concerned. (I seem to have learned quite a lot of Latin and Greek.)

8   *Eugen to Franz*

September 13, 1916

Dear Fellow (Jew + post-Christum natum + post-Hegel mortuum)![50]

Let's first of all unite in love of one person, namely Hermann

---

[48] Paul Siebeck, a publisher.
[49] Georg Mehlis, colleague of Franz Rosenzweig.
[50] Dear Fellow (Jew after Christ's birth and the death of Hegel)!

Cohen. I once traveled by train with him at night, and since then he often stands plainly before my eyes as a man to be reverenced. Hence, it was not *Cohen imprimens* but *Cohen impressus*[51] who was meant and scolded in my letter (I no longer recall quite how). On that occasion he sat opposite me during the evening and said several times to his wife—gloriously surprised, like a child before a Christmas tree—"How lovely, I'm not at all tired, I'm not at all tired!" There he was: the scholar, the fighter, the Jew all discarded—for all his seventy years a blessed, childlike person, who had been enraptured by the sweetness of divine life.——

To continue: do you really believe that the sort of love that you have for him is or could be a merely private affair?[52] Perhaps it is the one thing treasured in your soul, in our souls indeed, that can't remain a private affair. True, everything else makes you a private person, but in this particular case one keeps the secret that everyone must have for himself in order to be able to share with others. To illustrate this quite soberly in history: the proposition *cuius regio eius religio*[53] has become that of "Religion is a private affair," by an error similar to the one that caused the royal house to be displaced by Hegel's princely individual. Both propositions were intended to mean the emancipation of the individual through the addition of the word "private" and they have, thereby, checkmated him, because they have turned private affairs into isolated matters to be kept secret. Theoretically, this is what is said in Nathan: "Let each be zealous on his own account . . . ."[54] But in practice the order of life did

[51] Not as "Cohen impressing me" but as "Cohen in print."

[52] On January 17, 1920 Franz wrote to his fiancée that Eugen's wrath had fought Franz' attempt to call the real experiences purely "private," but that now he (Franz) knew that they were the only ones who had the right to make history (*Briefe*, p. 386).

[53] The principle of the Reformation: "The prince of a country determines the country's religion."

[54] "Therefore let each one imitate this love;
 So free from prejudice, let each one aim
 To emulate his brethren in the strife
 To prove the virtues of his several ring,
 By offices of kindness and of love, and trust in God."
—Lessing, *Nathan the Wise* (act III, scene 7).

everything to make this *arcanum*[55] of the individual into an
ἄδυτον [56] that cannot be entered by *anybody*—not even by the
individual himself. His shyness about this private affair becomes
pathological; one deprives him to such an extent that he neither
cares for nor enters his *arcanum*—and so one day he no longer
possesses it. Just as freedom *of* conscience, instead of leading to
an impetuous competition of consciences, became freedom *from*
conscience, so private religion leads to privation of religion,
though it is the number 1 for the 2–5 of your painter, and though
it is the source of all expression and form—"the way to salvation."
Thus, what is today private—apparently emancipated, but actually maimed—is at the same time the most decisive matter, the
individual character, i.e. the meaning of this our life, in which,
after all, the individual still has his say. So then, even if you have
made me very happy with your last letter and your antistrophe
to my *solo solissimo*,[57] I must still insist on considering just these
very "private matters" to be the most important of all.

.   .   .   .

As regards the Fathers, I can only help you provisionally, with
a catalogue from which you will perhaps find references to the
original texts. For the scholastics, St. Thomas in the Leonine Edition is temporarily unobtainable because it is published in Italy
(at least I tried to obtain it myself in vain three months ago). The
early Scholastics are comparatively inexpensive in Migne's *Patrologia*; you can get a big volume of a thousand pages for some
10 to 14 marks (St. Bernard, Peter Lombard, and so on, up to
1200. The last of the series is Innocent III).

I sent Spemann and Lippert as two halves of one whole. And
if you want to read something remarkable as well, read Heim
(professor in Münster), *Leitfaden der Dogmatik*,[58] 2nd edition
1916, N.B. a thin volume! (It is extremely compressed, but all the
more attractive for that.) He comes very near the truth. As far
as my Calendar is concerned, I am now keeping totally quiet.

You are also presently to receive two halves of one whole from

---

[55] Innermost sanctuary.
[56] Inner sanctuary, in the sense of a shrine that must not be entered.
[57] Most private utterance.
[58] Karl Heim's Guide to Dogmatics.

me myself—namely, a historical half and a polemical half. But I am waiting until I can send them together.

Look here!—as one can't see any end to the war—can't you have *Hegel und der Staat* published, if only for the sake of promotion? Even that leaves nothing for 1917. But I'm repeating all through my letter just what you yourself write.

Remain friends with your Eugen Rosenstock

9 *Franz to Eugen*

[no date]

Dear R.,

Cohen isn't an article of faith with me; my respect for him is very much as you describe yours. I had no suspicion that you felt like that, so I had a strong impulse not to let what you said go unchallenged, though there was no question of disproving it, especially because it was concerned with a purely private experience (like the railway journey at night). It is only that my experience goes still further, and I have detected this pure, strong, human quality also in the utterances of the "scholar, the fighter, and the Jew." Despite this, his philosophy, his politics, his Judaism are for me quite unimportant; but all the same, even if he has no philosophy, he is nonetheless the first full-blown professor I have seen whom, without mockery, I would call a philosopher. And it is the same with his Judaism.

So Cohen is a "private affair." We might now perhaps say two people's "private affair," but nevertheless still their private affair.

But you don't want to talk about Cohen, but about the ass that carries the bag.[59] And here, from the outset, I grant you— (I had almost said "obviously," but that would be unfair, because it is only thanks to you that it is obvious to me today)—well then, I grant you frankly everything that you say about the public side of religion, right up to the details of your way of putting it.

---

[59] An allusion to a German proverb to the effect that one beats the bag but aims at the ass in it. Franz meant that the correspondents should stop discussing Cohen (who was *in* the bag of Judaism) and turn to himself, as a bearer of the Jewish faith.

I have also lived like that since then, and I can say that it is only since then that I know what life—life with people—means. (Also, I only know since then what the burden of life means.) Only, don't you grumble about the Enlightenment; it is not its fault that inertia stuffed its discoveries into cushions, instead of industrious people getting to work on them. I believe, too, that I have intruded on you since our correspondence began. But what you miss, or rather what offends ($\sigma\kappa\alpha\nu\delta\alpha\lambda\iota\zeta\epsilon\iota$)[60] you, is that I do not expressly tell you (or perhaps after your talk with Rudi, merely confirm) that such and such, this and that, is the bond between your correspondent and the Jew.

You have made too light of it before (the $\sigma\kappa\alpha\nu\delta\alpha\lambda o\nu$[61] is an old story with you), because you simply put "the Jew" in inverted commas and lay him on one side as a kind of personal idiosyncracy, or at best, as a pious romantic relic of the posthumous influence of a dead great-uncle.[62] You make it difficult for us both, because you ask me to lay bare a skeleton that can only prove through its organic life that flesh and blood grow and flow round it. You can force a living being to commit this anatomical Hara-kiri simply from a moralistic compulsion and not from friendly interest; you did once rightly compel me to do it in Leipzig in 1913, when you would not seriously believe me, and did not allow anything I said to be really my own words, until I myself was horrified at how rotten was my flesh and how torpid my blood; then I myself had to turn to an examination of my anatomy. This time you have taken a different attitude from the outset, and I think you had a right to do so. When things were otherwise, when during these last years I was confronted with a spirit of naïve but passionate distrust, then I instinctively, immediately, reenacted that Hara-kiri, and so every time convinced my opponent insofar as he was capable of being convinced. But now you are not forcing me, and secondly (I must say it, however reluctantly), you are directly hindering me from treating my Judaism in the first person, in that you call yourself a Jew too. That is to me equally intolerable, emotionally and intellec-

[60] To give offense to, or cause difficulties for.
[61] A stumbling block; offense.
[62] Adam Rosenzweig (1826–1908).

tually. For me you can be nothing else but a Christian; the emptiest Jew, cut off root and branch and a Jew only in the legal sense, is still an object of concern to me as a Jew, but you are not. Moreover, suppose you were really a Christian ἐκ τῆς περιτομῆς[63] (you are one, but, in spite of your brilliant Logion of Luke,[64] only in your theoretical consciousness, not in the reality of your life before you were a Christian; and I know that now because I know your parents' house). But even if you were one, it would not make any difference to me, because I do not recognize this missionary–theological concept of "Christians from Israel," because it is positive and the Jew between the Crucifixion and the Second Coming can only have a negative meaning in Christian theology. The Jew κατ' ἐξοχήν,[65] the "Ahasuerus"[66] of Christian —and naturally Teutonic—lore is so everlastingly necessary a being for the yet militant Church that the missions can only work on individuals (to want to christianize the "eternal Jew" would be a blasphemy, a veritable "taking of the Kingdom of God by violence," a real βιάζεσθαι τὴν βασιλείαν τοῦ Θεοῦ[67]), whereas history shows that missions to heathen peoples are only in appearance directed to individuals; the Germans were not converted at the Aller[68] but in the Wartburg in 1521[69] ("without prejudice" —you as a medievalist will name other dates, but that is irrelevant). This may incidentally be a consolation to those who are

[63] From the circumcision.

[64] A reference to the unauthorized saying of Jesus connected with Luke 6:5, and frequently quoted by Eugen, that a man who breaks the Sabbath is blessed if he knows what he is doing, accursed if he does not. Franz alluded to it here in order to express a man's liberty to choose another way of faith. The saying appears in Luke 6:5 in the *Codex Bezae* (or *Cantabrigensis*) MS, one of two early MSS used by Theodore Beza (1519–1605) in preparing his 1565 edition of the New Testament in Greek.

[65] *Par excellence.*

[66] The "Wandering Jew" of medieval legend was a cobbler who refused to let Christ rest at his door while He was bearing the cross to Calvary, for which churlishness Ahasuerus was condemned to "tarry" on earth until Christ's second coming.

[67] To force the Kingdom of God.

[68] Referring to the baptism of the Saxon tribe at the River Aller.

[69] Luther's breaking away from the papacy.

honestly shocked over the alliance with Turkey. So this individual Jew—we also know from experience—as an individual, cut loose from his people (for the missionary can't possibly catch him so long as he is still a member in the "body" [σῶμα]—I am putting it in this way for you on purpose)—this individual Jew does not become a Christian *as a Jew*, but if he becomes one after heart-searching, and does not slip over imperceptibly, merely as the last step in a natural development is received as *nothing*, that is to say, just as it were as a heathen, but as a heathen before the Fall. So if for once I may permissibly stir up together Paul and Isocrates (quite permissibly, as expressing ἐκκλησία[70] and οἰκουμένη,[71] the Christian gospel and the Monumentum Ancyranum[72]), he is received not as ῞Ελλην ἐκ τῶν ῾Ελλήνων,[73] but as ῞Ελλην ἐκ τῶν βαρβάρων.[74] For him the preaching of the Cross was not really a stumbling block, for he was never a Jew (what do you know about that! What can you know about it! But I recognize my feeling in the merest remnant of a Jew and in the narrowest orthodox, a feeling which might be expressed in a gesture but hardly perhaps in words). Nor was the Cross really foolishness, since as I am here presenting him he was never properly a Greek, but to him it is as if it were the first word of God at the Creation. Thus there is a Christian naïveté in such people, a Johannine desire to take the world for a *mundus naturaliter christianus*[75]—the less they were ἐκ τῶν ῾Ελλήνων before, the more is this the case (and so to take examples, you find it in Neander[76] more than in Stahl,[77] and in Stahl more than in you). You see, and this is my point, how the distinction of Christians

[70] Church.
[71] The inhabited world.
[72] A famous Latin inscription, on the inside of the antae of the Temple of Augustus, giving a laudatory account of this emperor's deeds.
[73] A Greek from among Greeks.
[74] A Greek among barbarians.
[75] A world that is by nature Christian.
[76] Johann August Wilhelm Neander (1789–1850), a famous Lutheran (converted in 1806) theologian who encouraged the study of church history, and taught at the Universities of Heidelberg and Berlin.
[77] Friedrich Julius Stahl (1802–1861), a reactionary politician best known for his book *Die Philosophie des Rechts* . . . (1830–37), in which he sought to prove that Law and the State were of divine origin.

"from the Gentiles" and "from the circumcision" has today—
that is, after Christianity has emerged from its birth struggle and
not yet reached its deathbed—become Isocrates' distinction of
Ἕλλην and βάρβαρος[78] and has nothing more to do with the
Pauline distinction of Ἰουδαῖος and Ἕλλην.[79]

The Spemann came (not the Lippert) and I have already sent
it on to Rudi, to punish him because it is his fault I got it, and I
didn't care for it much, and I am very glad to gather from you
that it is only intended to be a first half. (You seem to regard it
as an extreme specimen of Protestant eschatology, in contrast to
an extreme specimen of Catholic eschatology—since Lippert appears to me to be an S.J.?). Apart from his distortion of the future after the Protestant manner, which explains (in direct challenge to Romans 11) that queer unloading of the Church as a
task onto the converted Jewish people in order that Christianity
until the Second Coming should have nothing to do but be
tempted and divided from the world, and leave it to the busy and
industrious People of God to do the rest—quite apart from this,
the superficiality of these pious people, who are supposed to be
learned, offends me. They move in an atmosphere where the
logical and metaphysical *salto mortale*[80] is the normal method of
progress, and they make use of it (naturally! otherwise how
could they get on!), but at the same time they wear such harmless
clerical faces that they look as if they were not making *salti
mortali*[81] through empty space, but playing leapfrog in a mea-
dow. To make the *salto* without the consciousness of empty
space is the privilege of the creative eschatologists in the moments
when they found religions. But in their case there is no suspicion
that they are playing leapfrog; they are moving between heaven
and earth; only heaven hangs close over the earthly atmosphere
like a veil. But the man who knows in his heart about empty
space is telling lies when he plays leapfrog.

Just as I had got so far, and had succeeded in saying what I
wanted to say (since the man who seeks for truth takes on him-

[78] Hellenic (Greek) and barbarian.
[79] Jew and Greek.
[80] Decisive or crucial leap.
[81] Decisive or crucial leaps.

self the obligation to make the correct scholarly approach), the mail came and brought first the promised catalogue (Kösel's *Kirchenväter*,[82] which I suspected might come) and second, the Lippert,[83] which I immediately began—and it was so good that I finished it the same evening. So that was the other half? The first eschatology, the second organization? It is indeed most remarkable, and I was not fully aware before, that eschatology exists today in Protestantism as a free power and source of possibilities, whereas it really exists in Catholicism only as it is bound up with and built into its structure. The Catholic Church also has become sectless only because of the second schism. Protestantism, in breaking away, has taken away with it, like a robber, the power of building sects and heresies. But all the same, even an eschatology in bonds remains an eschatological force, just as in an already militarized people it is their strength that carries on the war. The problem that Lippert solves with classical elegance, namely to show how an organization can be a soul, is something I have always seized on involuntarily with regard to the Jesuit Order whenever I read anything about them, as lately in the very beautiful little book by Böhmer, which is in the proper sense of the word rich in matter ("The Jesuits," in the series *Aus Natur und Geisteswelt*[84]). Now I am eager for Heim.

Your recommending Migne has moved me to tears—one volume in each trouser pocket, one tied up in the tail of my battle charger, two more in my saddle bags—but no, the beasts aren't getting any more oats—vanish dream!

Vanish also second dream, that *Hegel und der Staat* could be published in its present state of preparation. The book must still cost me three months of full days' work, and since I shall not be able to have them, six months of half-days. It will then not read very differently from the way it does now, but it will be more commodious in the cellar and safer in the beams. The reader is only a visitor in a book; the man who accidentally or purposely

[82] Josef Kösel's Fathers of the Church.

[83] Father Peter Lippert's *Zur Psychologie des Jesuitnordens* (Psychology of the Jesuit Order).

[84] On Nature and the Spiritual World.

has worked over a bit of it knows it like the house that one has rented and lived in.

But the war is no longer "incalculable." Since the entry of Rumania a phrase has been at the back of my mind that expresses something I have already several times since said in plain prose, because in plain prose it is appropriate to this lengthening and twisting of the front, and is realized by the opening of the Dobrudska offensive. Today the proper phrase came to me in its proper form, and I can write it down for you: "Wo aber Gefahr ist, wächst das Rettende auch—."[85] The war has become calculable.

Your   Franz Rosenzweig

10   *Eugen to Franz*

October 4, 1916

Dear Franz,

You give me every time a veritable breakfast of caviar. I know people, indeed, with whom one can be concerned with truth and find truth, but "truth" in a form corresponding to the present position of scholarship: that is something only the learned can enjoy, and it is therefore a rare treat. Moreover, you overestimate, unfortunately, the Christian in me. I am not Paul of Tarsus—unfortunately not. Before you my mission comes to a halt. You are the human individual, one whose particular quality I recognize in spite of his being "outside Christianity." I see Judaism just as you prescribe it to the "Church"—and to yourself— as for me, the revelation of God in the world from day to day, from being a mere abstract, metaphorical conception in the background, becomes more and more a present reality here and now. The Jews are so much the chosen people, and the Old Testament is so much the book of the law of the Father, just as the New is the book of the love of the children, (Abraham and Christ, sacrifice the two poles, on the one hand the Father, on the other the Son), that altogether the Church needs "its" Jews

[85] A line from one of Hölderlin's poems, meaning: "But where there is danger, that which saves also grows.

to strengthen its own truth. The stubbornness of the Jews is, so to speak, a Christian dogma. But is it, can it also be, a Jewish one? That is the fence that I do not see you taking. On this point I am completely unable to understand you and—I won't disturb you, but you alone of all men in the world. So now I am amazed that you suspect a "Jewish will" or something like it in my reflections. My parents' home, like yours, finds itself in a state of self-disintegration, with its good-natured worship of cleverness. But let's leave out personal considerations of this kind. If you would attribute to me a *visio mundi naturaliter christiani*,[86] I am sensible that this expression stood, in its time, for something true. My strongest experience in the war is, however, precisely the turning, step by step, of the natural into the unnatural. Today for myself, as E. R., as a *naturalis doctor*[87] and *locumtenens regius*,[88] the Cross is a stumbling-block and folly. And I believe that that uncompromising "revolt," the position of Kierkegaard, will be getting stronger. But it is still a long way to Kierkegaard, that grim and grisly monster without confession and so without Church, and there is nothing to point me in that direction.

Why then do you dialectical thinkers[89] want to confront nature with the same Either–Or, which is only valid for salvation in that you analyze whether I, o (zero) am Ἕλλην ἐκ τῶν βαρβάρων[90] or ἐκ τῆς περιτομῆς,[91] and so on? Do you think that one must be able to establish this so unambiguously with regard to one man, a baptized or unbaptized Jewish doctor of a German university? The mixture of Goethe and Wilhelm Busch[92] would be a modest salad in comparison.

In respect of one part of me, I presume to judge myself as pre-Christian Jewish racial material. In my capacity for suffering and in my craving for it, the Jew comes out. I forge together Ger-

[86] A vision of a world naturally Christian.

[87] A teacher of that which relates to nature.

[88] The king's "lieutenant" literally is *locumtenens*, placeholder, substitute of the king.

[89] Cf. references to Hegelian dialectics in Letter No. 16 (p. 139), and see note 174 (p. 147).

[90] A Greek among barbarians.

[91] From the circumcision.

[92] A satirical poet.

man and Jewish gifts and possessions in my attempt to become a Christian. This is my quite uncritical view of myself. And, as I said before, my attitude to you remains quite incomprehensible to me; it is not indifferent and yet is tolerant, and I am content to ask myself, with Cyrano: "Que diable allait-il faire dans cette galère ——?"[93]

We have been in four theaters of war within two months! I am nibbling at Kant as the last of the scholastics. I'm afraid it can't be helped: my "Calendar of the common sense male understanding" is going to attack nothing less than His Excellency the Critique of Pure Reason. Have you read Rüdorffer's[94] book on Nationality? I am now reading one of his Kantian authorities, also a young man, who even before the war was sensing the change of intellectual outlook, and had entered on the threshold of the new world. It is dreadful to see how such a "natural," subjectively isolated mind suffers and stammers, even and particularly at the very point where he approaches the truth. The book is called Kurt Riezler, *Die Erforderlichkeit des Unmöglichen, Prolegomena zu einer Theorie der Politik,*[95] 1913. What a veritable hell of timeless, wordless, and contentless abstractions these Gorlands, Riezlers, Kroners,[96] etc. bring to light! And I am sometimes shocked at the way the Schools have laid waste the noblest of human powers. The root of the scholastic and Kantian errors seems to me to be quickly indicated: they take the truths in which logic is embodied as "purely logical" truths in opposition to others in which logic is *not* embodied. I would like to go through Kant's Critiques just to see how far, sentence by sentence, they themselves are metaphysical in their formal rhetor-

---

[93] A reference to the *Pedant Joué* of Cyrano de Bergerac, imitated by Molière in *Les fourberies de Scapin* (act II, scene 11). The father, when told that his son has been kidnapped by the Turks on a galley, keeps repeating: "Que diable allait-il faire dans cette galère?" This motif of the galley (in this case standing for Judaism) recurs in later passages of the correspondence.

[94] See note 112.

[95] The Demand of the Impossible, Prolegomena to a Theory of Politics. See note 112.

[96] Members of a neo-Kantian school.

ical, illogical structure. Do you know *Fechner*???[97] The quickest introduction is his *Tagesansicht im Gegensatz zur Nachtansicht*,[98] a legacy from a man of seventy-eight. You will find it less successful as a cosmology than as a—or more correctly, as *the*—phenomenology (the only one in the nineteenth century) that can heal the "torn-apart" (= abstractum) thinking of the Schools. It makes it all the funnier that Ẇundt,[99] in the introduction to his master's little book about the life after death, says that the reader can find everything in Fechner except a theory of knowledge. The pupil–schoolmaster was so astonished by the system that he had no idea that in all of it Fechner was going his own way subjectively, abstractly, arbitrarily, and that all that will remain as his immense merit is his having formulated once more in a clear, simple, lay manner the right to have a system— and that is, in fact, a theory of knowledge.

Do you know Wundt's *Völkerpsychologie*?[100] One more of the death spasms of Protestantism. A collection of religions undergo review, and Christianity is defended victoriously against Buddhism. All primitive peoples are considered. But with the year 30 the history of religions came to an end, only to be taken up again about 1870, from when onwards it advocates a creedless cult as the goal of Christianity. A philosopher in 1915, when this book appeared, "proves" compellingly that one ought to retain no compulsory elements in religious faith because—nothing can be proved. And these artists in vicious circles look down on a mind like Mauthner's, who only draws the consequence, and

[97] Gustav Theodor Fechner (1801–1887), founder of "psychophysics."

[98] The Aspect of Day in Contrast to the Aspect of Night.

[99] Wilhelm Max Wundt (1832–1920), founder of experimental psychology.

[100] This famous work (2 vols., 1900; 1905–1906) is available in English, but under the misleading title *Folk-psychology* (1916). "Psychology of Nations" (nations in the sense of "peoples") would be a more accurate translation. It includes his most important discovery, one having to do with the relation of word and sentence: logically and historically, he found, sentences *precede* words, and thus a complete spiritual act is presupposed by all its parts. Further, Wundt acknowledged the need of *all* men—even scientists—for myth. Unfortunately, Wundt failed to develop these insights adequately.

proves the incomprehensibility and incommunicability of all
thinking and of all language in the course of a work in three
volumes.[101] A Spaniard was lately asked by a member of the
Entente why he preferred German *"Kultur"* to Parisian *"genie."*
His answer was: "I prefer letting myself be boxed on the ears
by a schoolmaster like Wundt, to being made a fool of by a
juggler like Bergson."

Do you know Gobineau?[102] If not, let yourself be sent everything of his that is in Reclam's edition.

You will perhaps be annoyed that I have used your plenary
powers to write on your behalf to Rickert about the Schelling
essay. You would certainly not have roused yourself to do it of
your own accord.

In Conflans I was to read "Church and State" for eighteen
hours. That is, I had been appointed to give lectures on political
philosophy and constitutional history within the syllabus of the
wartime higher education courses,[103] and was allowed to define
the subject for myself *ad libitum* under cover of this. I am la-
menting that I could not "occupy" this new territory; we are
leaving here.

Goodbye.　Yours, E.R.

11　*Franz to Eugen*

Dear R.,

I want to begin to answer you at once. (I got your letter yes-

[101] This work, which went through several editions in Germany, was
Beiträge zu einer Kritik der Sprache, first published in 1901–1902, by Fritz
Mauthner (1849–1923), a radical skeptic of the day. "Fritz Mauthner wrote
6000 pages and proved in one and a half million words that all words lie.
And he got his books printed and they are in all the libraries of the world
because in their heart of hearts, all academic people treat languages as rudi-
ments of a barbaric age. How they would prefer to think without words!"
(from Eugen's essay "A Horse Block" [1945], now printed in *Die Sprache
des Menschengeschlechts* [Heidelberg: Verlag Lambert Schneider, 1963–
1964], vol. 1, p. 23–31).

[102] Comte Josephe de Gobineau (1816–1882), among other things a no-
torious anti-Semitic race theorist.

[103] The Army group von Strantz organized lecture courses for the
troops.

terday. I was thinking that the 103rd Division would perhaps have come to Mackensen, and my letter would have had to make the journey twice over.) I am suffering from a paper shortage as you see.

Our present correspondence is suffering from the fact that on the one hand we could not put it off, while on the other hand it is still too soon for it. I can see that very clearly, because I am the one who was responsible for the long gap (of the winter of 1913–1914). I could not write to you then, though you were continually sounding me and were offended because of my silence. I could not, because I thought I had done with you as you were up to then, and as I had dug you out at the end of our time in Leipzig, up to certain undiscoverable fragments (I won't say which parts of your body), put you together, and exhibited you in my museum in a gallery on a revolving pedestal, with a piece of dark blue stuff, which made a good background to you. That you were walking about alive despite this statue was almost an insult to me. I had to ignore it, and to appease my pangs of conscience with the idea that I had "put the matter off." That you were in fact walking about very much alive I realized, of course, when you were in Berlin in the spring, but I didn't feel myself strong enough, not indeed physically, but spiritually, to challenge you all over again (since it would only have been done as a challenge, and will so be done again); to my mind I was not actual enough, not tested enough, not enough on the spot, and to me there would have been no point in a merely theoretical controversy. Formerly, I had confronted you as a point of view, as an objective fact, and you were the first to summon me to an analysis of myself, and thereby cast me down. I would have liked to wait until I could again confront you as a *fait accompli*. 'Till then we could have kept our guest rooms ready for each other, and put some little cheap flowers in them as a token of our feeling for one another. That does, and would have done.

"Then the War came." And with it came a time of waiting against one's will, a chasm that one does not make artificially for oneself, but that was opened blindly in every life; and now it is no longer any good to wait deliberately; fate is now so calmly patient with individuals (from indifference towards them, because it has its hands full with nations) that we individuals ought just now to be impatient, unless we want simply to go to sleep (for fate certainly won't wake us up now). So now we are talking to each other theoretically, *faute de mieux*. But for that reason everything that we say to each other is incomplete, not incomplete like the flow of life that completes itself anew in every moment, but full of static incompletenesses, full of distortions.

You "leave me alone." You "don't know why." You "stop at me." Nevertheless, I reply and give you an answer that is theoretically correct, interesting, and I'm sure you will agree with it. You want to know what business I have on that galley[104]—but it were better you did not agree, did not know, but *just saw me set sail on that galley* without knowing what business I had on it, rather than that *my galley should now be lying idle in a neutral port since the beginning of the war*, and that I should incur your intellectual sympathy, since the *vis major* of the war prevents me from acquiring your active hatred; for there is in the delay the danger of indifference, which lies beyond love and hate, and that would be the worst of all.

Now to the point. You could have formulated your objection still more strongly; I should like perhaps later to do it for you. But first let's stick to your formulation. Yes, the stubbornness of the Jews is a Christian dogma. So much so that the Church, after she had built up the substantial part of her particular dogma— the part having to do with God and Man—in the first century, during the whole of the second century turned aside to lay down the "second dogma" (the formal part of her dogma, i.e. her historical consciousness of herself). And in its aftereffects this process continued through the third and fourth centuries and beyond; and Augustine applied himself to it personally, though the Church had already for some time been moving away from it. That is, it had been becoming a Church of writings or rather of tradition, instead of spirit; in other words, it was becoming exactly the Church that history knows. Paul's theory concerning the relation of the Gospels to the Law could have remained a

[104] See note 93.

"personal opinion"; the Hellenizing "spiritual" Church (of John's Gospel) of the first century, in the marvelous naïveté of her "spiritual believers," had scarcely worried about it. Then came gnosticism, which laid its finger on Paul and sought to weed out the personal element from his theory and to develop its objective aspects in distinction from the personal in it. (Paul said: "The Jews are spurned, but Christ came from them." Marcion said: "Therefore the Jews belong to the devil, Christ to God.") Then the Church, which hitherto had been quite naïve in its own gnosticism (in St. John we read that salvation comes from the Jews), suddenly seeing this, pushed the spirit [pneuma] to one side in favor of tradition, and through a great *ritornar al segno* fixed this tradition by returning to its cardinal point, to its founder Paul; that is, she deliberately established as dogma what previously had been considered Paul's personal opinion. The Church established the identity of the Creator (and the God revealed at Sinai) with the Father of Jesus Christ on the one hand, and the perfect manhood of Christ on the other hand, as a definite, correlated Shibboleth against all heresy—and thereby the Church established herself as a power in human history. You know the rest better than I do. (N.B. I have just read all this in Tertullian, of whom I bought a complete edition dating from the thirties of the last century for two marks. I warn you against it emphatically! For the first and last time, as a result of pure folly and stinginess, I am reading an as-good-as-uncollated text. I know now at last why the textual critic is necessary. Scarcely any sentence is understandable; one has to guess at the meaning paragraph by paragraph, though I have a feeling for Tertullian's style. I prefer his rhetoric, as that of a real lawyer, to the professorial rhetoric of Augustine, just because it is more genuine— at least according to our modern ideas.)

Thus, in the firm establishment of the Old Testament in the Canon, and in the building of the Church on this double scripture (Old Testament and New Testament) the stubbornness of the Jews is in fact brought out as the other half of the Christian dogma (its formal consciousness of itself—the dogma of the Church—if we may point to the creed as the dogma of Christianity).

But could this same idea (that of the stubbornness of the Jews) also be a Jewish dogma? Yes, it could be, and in fact it is. But this Jewish consciousness of being rejected has quite a different place in our dogmatic system, and would correspond to a Christian consciousness of being chosen to rule, a consciousness that is in fact present beyond any doubt. The whole religious interpretation of the significance of the year 70[105] is tuned to this note. But the parallel that you are looking for is something entirely different. A dogma of Judaism about its relation to the Church must correspond to the dogma of the Church about its relation to Judaism. And this you know only in the form of the modern liberal-Jewish theory of the "daughter religion" that gradually educates the world for Judaism. But this theory actually springs from the classical period in the formation of Jewish dogma—from the Jewish high scholasticism which, in point of time and in content, forms a mean between Christian and Arabian scholasticism (al-Ghazali–Maimonides–Thomas Aquinas). For it was only then that we had a fixing of dogma, and that corresponds with the different position that intellectual conceptions of faith hold with us and with you. In the period when you were developing dogma, we were creating our canon law, and vice versa. There is a subtle connection running all through. For instance, when you were systematizing dogma, we were systematizing law; with you the mystical view of dogma followed its definition, while with us the mystical view preceded definition, etc., etc. This relation is rooted throughout in the final distinction between the two faiths. Indeed with us, too, this theory is not part of the substance of our dogma; with us, too, it was not formed from the content of the religious consciousness but belongs only to a second stratum, a stratum of learning concerning dogma. The theory of the daughter religion is found in the clearest form in both of the great scholastics. Beyond this, it is found, not as dogma but as a mystical idea (see above), in the literature of the old Synagogue, and likewise in the Talmudic period. To find it is no easy task, however. For whereas the substantial dogma in our scholasticism was based on trials, the connection between the old

---

[105] That is, the traditional date of the destruction of the Temple.

mysticism and medieval philosophy is brought about by the free religious spirit of the people, not by a fettered relationship to the past. But I should like to quote you one such legend. The Messiah was born exactly at the moment when the Temple was destroyed, but when he was born, the winds blew him forth from the bosom of his mother. And now he wanders unknown among the peoples, and when he has wandered through them all, then the time of our redemption will have come.

So that Christianity is like a power that fills the world (according to the saying of one of the two scholastics, Yehuda ha-Levi: it is the tree that grows from the seed of Judaism and casts its shadows over the earth; but its fruit must contain the seed again, the seed that nobody who saw the tree noticed. This is a Jewish dogma, just as Judaism as both the stubborn origin and last convert is a Christian dogma.

But what does all that mean for me, apart from the fact that I know it? What does this Jewish dogma mean for the Jew? Granted that it may not belong to the dogmas of the substantial group, which like the corresponding Christian dogmas can be won from an analysis of the religious consciousness. It is rather like the corresponding Christian one, a theological idea. But theological ideas must also mean something for religion. What, then, does it mean?

What does the Christian theological idea of Judaism mean for the Christian? If I am to believe E. R.'s letter before last (or before the one before the last?): Nothing! For there he wrote that nowadays König and he are the only people who still take Judaism seriously. The answer is already on the point of my pen— that it was not here a question of theoretical awareness, but whether there was a continual realization of this theological idea by its being taken seriously in actual practice. This practical way, in which the theological idea of the stubbornness of the Jews works itself out, is *hatred of the Jews*. You know as well as I do that all its realistic arguments are only fashionable cloaks to hide the single true metaphysical ground: that we will not make common cause with the world-conquering fiction of Christian dogma, because (however much a fact) it *is* a fiction (and "*fiat veritas, pereat realitas,*"[106] since "Thou God art truth") and, putting it in a learned way (from Goethe in *Wilhelm Meister*): that we deny the foundation of contemporary culture (and "*fiat regnum Dei, pereat mundus,*"[107] for "ye shall be to me a kingdom of priests and a holy people"); and putting it in a popular way: that we have crucified Christ and, believe me, would do it again every time, we alone in the whole world (and "*fiat nomen Dei Unius, pereat homo,*"[108] for "to whom will you liken me, that I am like?").

And so the corresponding Jewish outcome of the theological idea of Christianity as a preparer-of-the-way is the *pride of the Jews*. This is hard to describe to a stranger. What you see of it appears to you silly and petty, just as it is almost impossible for the Jew to see and judge anti-Semitism by anything but its vulgar and stupid expressions. But (I must say again, *believe me*) its metaphysical basis is, as I have said, the three articles: (1) that we have the truth, (2) that we are at the goal, and (3) that any and every Jew feels in the depths of his soul that the Christian relation to God, and so in a sense their religion, is particularly and extremely pitiful, poverty-stricken, and ceremonious; namely, that as a Christian one has to learn from someone else, whoever he may be, to call God "our Father." To the Jew, that God is our Father is the first and most self-evident fact—and what need is there for a third person between me and my father in Heaven? That is no discovery of modern apologetics but the simplest Jewish instinct, a mixture of failure to understand and pitying contempt.

These are the two points of view, both narrow and limited just as points of view, and so in theory both can be surpassed; one can understand why the Jew can afford his unmediated closeness to God and why the Christian may not; and one can also understand how the Jew must pay for this blessing. I can elaborate this argument in extreme detail. It can be intellectualized through and through, for it springs in the last resort from

---

[106] Let there be truth, and let reality perish.
[107] Let there be the kingdom of God, and let the world pass away.
[108] Let the name of One God exist, and let man pass away.

that great victorious breaking in of the spirit into what is not spirit that one calls "Revelation."

But now I want to formulate your question in a way that seems profitable to me—but is not such intellectualizing, as an activity of knowing, preparing, acting on the future, like every cultural activity, a Christian affair, not a Jewish affair? Are you still a Jew in that you do it? Is not part of the price that the Synagogue must pay for the blessing in the enjoyment of which she antici-pates the whole world, namely, of being already in the Father's presence, that she must wear the bandages of unconsciousness over her eyes? Is it sufficient if you carry the broken staff in your hand, as you do—I am willing to believe it—and yet take the bandages away from your eyes?

Here the polished clarity of antitheses ends; here begins the world of more and less, of compromise, of reality, or, as the Jewish mysticism of the late Middle Ages very finely said for "World of Reality, of Thinghood," "World of Activity, of Matter of Fact"; and as I should prefer to say, the "World of Action." Action alone can here decide for me, but even if it has decided for me, I still always need indulgence? Not as if thought is here entirely left behind; but it no longer goes as before along a proud, sure king's highway, with vanguard, flanks, and count-less trains of attendants; it goes lonely along the footpath in pilgrim dress. Something like this:

You recollect the passage in the Gospel of John where Christ explains to his disciples that they should not leave the world, but should remain within it. Even so, the people of Israel—who in-deed could use all the sayings of this Gospel—could speak to its members in such a way, and as a matter of fact it does so: "to hallow the name of God in the world," is a phrase that is often used. From this follows all the ambiguity of Jewish life (just as all the dynamic character of the Christian life follows from it). The Jew, insofar as he is "in the world," stands under these laws and no one can tell him that he is permitted to go just so far and no farther, or that there is a line that he may not cross. Such a simple "as little as possible" would be a bad standard, because if I wished to govern all of my actions by the standard "as little as possible from outside Judaism" it would mean, in the circumstances, a diminution of my inner Jewish achievement. So I say to myself as a rule: "as much as possible of the inner Jewish life"—though I well know that in the particular case I cannot anxiously avoid a degree of life outside Judaism. I also know that thereby, in your eyes, I open the way to a charge of soullessness. I can only answer fully at the center and source of my activity; at the periphery it escapes me. But should I then let the citadel fall in order to strengthen these precarious outworks? Should I "be converted," when I have been "chosen" from birth? Is that a real alternative for me? Have I only been thrown into the galley? Is it not *my* ship? You became acquainted with me on land, but you have scarcely noticed that my ship lies in harbor and that I spend more time than is necessary in sailors' taverns, and therefore you could well ask what business I have on the ship. And for you really to believe that it is my ship, and that I therefore belong to it (*pour faire quoi? y vivre et y mourir*)— for you really to believe me will only be possible if the voyage is once more free and I launch out.

Or only when we meet out on the open sea? You might!

Now from the *multum* to the *multa*[109] in your letter. I know Gobineau's book on the Renaissance, and possess without having read them the rest of his books in Reclam. Indeed "everyone" knows his Renaissance, just as "everyone" knows whatever is read by both sexes. Don't you think it is really a remarkable connection? Only what belongs in common to both man and woman belongs to *all* men, and everything else has only sectional interest. For instance, Hans Ehrenberg is now reading Lagarde[110] for the first time in his life. Incidentally, will you be seeing him some time? I don't know the geographical possibilities. He is in a sanatorium in Sedan. He is the strangest phenomenon of the war that I have come across, as far as people go. Everyone has in himself some extreme possibility that is in the highest degree typical of him, and in his case, through the war, and before that already of course through his very strange marriage, and before both of these, that is, before everything else, through his own

---

[109] The important matter . . . the many lesser matters.

[110] Paul Anton de Lagarde, née Bötticher (1827–1891), a noted Orientalist and anti-Semitic writer.

will to lead an extreme life, this possibility has become an actuality; he is now what might have been "lost" in him when he became a professor.[111]

Yes, I wouldn't have gone to Rickert with the Schelling essay—for personal reasons; but a thousand kilometres as the crow flies makes one enormously indifferent, so it is all right. But after the various rejections I certainly no longer trust your judgment and mine with respect to the value of the work.

Isn't Rüdorffer a pseudonym for Riezler? Anyhow, it is the pseudonym of "a man who stands very near the Chancellor." I have not read him yet. You mean, I take it, the *Weltpolitik der Gegenwart*[112] or is *Nationalität*[113] another, smaller book? Riezler is in the Foreign Office, and son-in-law of Max Liebermann.[114] It is so long since I had any cause to bother myself over the Kantians. Even when I was reading Kant himself (lately it was the *ewigen Frieden*,[115] and in February the *Religion innerhalb der Grenzen*[116]), I did not find any reason to turn to them. I mean the present "schools" have simply the significance of being schools. One must have passed through one of them—it doesn't matter which (I did the Southwest German one)—but afterwards one need only to bother himself further with the Master, the "good Master, long since dead." You indicate the fundamental attitude of the whole Kantian movement, just as Hans also does in his last writing ("last"—in 1911! And we used to take him for a man who was always rushing wildly into print). I was introduced

[111] Hans Ehrenberg (1883–1958), a cousin of Franz, commanded an infantry battalion in the war and at the time of this letter was probably enjoying a respite from the horrors of the battlefield. He had been a university professor before the war—hence Franz' reference to "what might have been 'lost' in him." His marriage in 1913 to Else Zimmermann and then the war turned him away from the narrowly academic way of life.

[112] Franz was of course correct in identifying "J. J. Rüdorffer" as a pseudonym of Kurt Riezler, the true author of *Grundzüge der Weltpolitik in der Gegenwart* (Foundations of World Politics in the Present Day), 1914.

[113] Nationality.

[114] The famous painter.

[115] Perpetual Peace.

[116] Religion within the Limits of Reason.

to Fechner in Bölsche's volume of essays, *Hinter der Welt-stadt*,[117] and by accident, I read the Zend-Avesta in my first term as a student. Up to then my knowledge of philosophy had been limited to: some of the first volume of Büttner's edition of Eckhart, Plato's Symposium, Schopenhauer's *Uber die Weiber*,[118] Nietzsche's *Der Fall Wagner*;[119] and I was quite captivated by Fechner (he describes, yes, really describes, the world as a great living being, and what is dead in it not as the source of life, but as an unburied corpse of what was formerly alive, since life is itself a source, and doesn't arise from anything else); subsequently, I have read only the little book *Vom Leben nach dem Tode*.[120] Wundt's relation to Fechner as a pupil is, I suppose, only in respect of his being the founder, as Fechner was, apart from everything else, the man who attempted to introduce mathematical methods into psychology (pure, not physiological psychology). Wundt, too, is one of the many people on whom I am not keen; I will look into all these matters as opportunity arises and when the *subject* inspires me (since the author will certainly leave me cold. Heim I am reading to the end just now; he is very good (but ought one not sometime to read M. Kähler himself?) I spent almost an entire week without reading anything, because I was writing something myself, namely, a syllabus for the school of the future!

Two missives were registered to me from your hand from Kassel, but they are not yet here. I discovered the little volume of poetry through a note from Klabund in the *Berliner Tageblatt*. Read it all the same.

And now a request. I have compressed my thoughts into tablet form for you, having regard for the weight restrictions of the field postal service and my paper shortage. If you pour on boiling water everyone can get a pint of strong coffee. So, requite me equal measure, and please explain to me your present idea of the relation between Nature and Revelation. That you have altered

[117] Behind the City of the World, by Wilhelm Bölsche (1861–1939), a novelist, translator, etc., who zealously propagated the theories of Charles Darwin and Ernst Haeckel.
[118] Concerning Women.
[119] The Case of Wagner.
[120] Of the Life after Death.

your opinion on this hasn't just happened during the war, but as long ago as the spring of 1914 you were using the concept "paganism" in your talk in a way that I could not understand. Where do you stand between the E. R. of the night of July 7, 1913 and Kierkegaard? I am asking so roundly and tactlessly because by those same round tablets of mine I have acquired a right at least to ask the question, if not also, I recognize, to obtain an answer. Heim's weakness, so far as I can see at present—I am on the border between the general and the Christian part of the book—as that of his whole circle, is that the history of philosophy ceases for him with Kant and as an alternative to the Idealists he knows only the specialist dogmatic theologians of the nineteenth century. Hence, he does not ask himself: How would it be if philosophy itself adopted the paradox[121] as its basis? But then he would have to concern himself with an immense task in the history of philosophy, and the beautiful short guides would no longer suffice (for, dear friend, only theory is short). Thus he has allowed the question of Christianity and philosophy (and with it, Christianity and the world) to be stultified in the simpler question of "Christianity and Paganism," and he still evades the particularly burning group of questions about the Christian world (Philosophy, Art, the State, Marriage, and so forth). But I want to read on further.

One further question. Has Speech no longer the meaning for you that it used to have? Could you express better what you mean by speaking about it? With cordial greetings, from "The sender" [N.B.: printed on the official letter form].

12　*Eugen to Franz*

October 28, 1916

Dear Franz,

You are right about your concentrated coffee extract. And if

[121] That is, the "paradox" in Kierkegaard's sense: how general and universal truth can be expressed in terms of existence, which is individual and historical.

I enjoy myself indescribably over such a letter, I realize how cursory and empty is my answer. Why didn't you come a year ago, or six months ago? Then I was charged up like a high tension wire. But at present I am like one of those damned batteries for pocket torches that you buy nowadays; and where there is nothing inside, friendship itself and the most heartfelt desire have lost their rights.

You have a way of asking me things in such a correct, impersonal way that I stand nonplussed. I have never been asked anything like that before, and so I do not know how to answer. Something occurs to me, and then something irritates me. That sets the ball rolling for my brain cells. In the end they emerge from their confusion. *C'est tout.* I don't think systematically, but from need, and I follow my needs one by one. And this temporal character in my thinking is in fact the Alpha and Omega from which I grasp everything afresh. Speech reflects this mode of procedure, even for someone who has been infected by philosophy. For that reason I used to prefer to talk about speech rather than about reason.

Nature and revelation: the same material, but opposite ways of being exposed to this light. The more everyday the material, the more revealing and revealed can it become. Only the contrivances and subjective ideas of man, their specialisms, cannot become revelation because they were not natural; but bread and wine can. Faith is a means that fully dwells only in the morally healthy and disintegrates and dissolves through impurity, and it is entirely comparable to a natural force. Christ has mediated to us the breaking through into the universe in a heavenward direction of this force, which was latent and imprisoned in the earth. Where hitherto was only Abraham's bosom, there is now a living eternity and an ascent of spirits from star to star. Revelation means the linking of our consciousness also with the union between earth and heaven that transcends the world. The question you put, "Nature and Revelation," I can only understand as "natural understanding" and revelation. Nature and Revelation are not comparable. Natural Understanding, then, knows front and back, left and right, and helps itself in this enclosure with a net of analogies. It makes comparisons and thus limps from one place to the next in this vast space. The lawyer is the perfect type of male understanding that with the help of an analogy can docket night as a particular case of day, and so, through a procession of leaps like the pilgrims of Echternach,[122] eventually reduce the world of phenomena to something so like a reflection of himself that the sun, moon, and stars themselves can be related to him. (N.B. Just as man through his comparisons embraces the most different of things, so woman through fashion makes what is everlastingly the same into the most different. Both are examples of lameness. No wonder, when you recognize that only what can be reached and known by man *and* woman can be a living universal good; and thereby it proves by limping on both sides that its method of progress is almost a human one.)

The resolution not to take one's own position in this quarter of space as the center of knowledge, but as conditioned from above—this renunciation of being ὀμφαλός κόσμου[123]—is no longer a matter of the natural human understanding, but is the means within us that makes revelation to, in, and for us possible. Schleiermacher's "absolute dependence," therefore, ought not to be comprehended in an external way as a feeling of fate, but should be understood as an illumination. However, since thought and speech constitute a continuous mutual relation of giving and receiving, and since both are a universal gift to the human race, for this twofold relation a double process is possible. You can believe in your autonomy. The Kantians believe in a senseless exaggeration of the autonomy of thought. The actual fact of seeing, on the contrary, testifies only to the autonomy of the married couple, speech *and* reason. For self-confidence of reason and trust in speech are both equally essential to a man who wants knowledge. But all such autonomous knowledge is without standards, supported only by experience, and without any δός μοι ποῦ στῶ.[124] I call this "luxuriating" thinking, for it be-

[122] A Benedictine cloister in Luxembourg where there is an annual procession of pilgrims called the "jumping procession." The pilgrims leap three steps forward and two back.

[123] The hub of the universe.

[124] The saying of Archimedes, declaring that he could weigh the world if he could take up his position at a point outside it, as a fulcrum.

haves like a weed. It doesn't die down. It comprehends gaily without any idea of there being a $\mu\acute{\epsilon}\tau\rho ον \pi\acute{α}ντων$,[125] and it is ingenuous about itself. This·kind of knowledge lives in all ages. It is of the people; I would rather say "people" for $\acute{\epsilon}θνος$ than pagan. It lives in the Middle Ages as strongly as it does today, and it sets itself in mighty waves against revelation and defends itself against the two swords—that of the Emperor as much as that of the Pope. Its mightiest outbreak is that of 1789. It has led to a complete undermining of Protestant Christianity, which today often threatens to become a mere theism without mediator, without conversion, without that bond from heaven to earth which makes space stable, like a rock of bronze, through the concept of *Above*. This theism stands on exactly the same level as that of primitive peoples. It is a survival without power, an echo of distant time, just as the fragments of civilization of those primitive peoples are today exposed as survivals and echoes. This natural folk belief in God is, then, an Old Testament without Testament and Law, in any case non- and pre-Christian. So I was right in 1914 to call it paganism.

This paganism is now dominant in all the Churches, insofar as science aspires to live "without presuppositions." You get it, above all, in Harnack, who is at the same time quite a man of faith, but also, unfortunately, a man who has more respect for science than he does for God and for God's Word. Now comes the crucial point. Speech, the $λόγος$[126] in all these peoples—the $\acute{\epsilon}θνη$ of antiquity, the nations of today—is imprisoned in itself, and it is, just for that reason, so completely ingenuous. It casts out the devil with Beelzebub, one analogy through the next, one comparison through a new image. All "natural" mind is metaphysical without knowing it. Because secretly it is frightened of its own powerlessness, of merely wriggling like a worm through the expanse of space, it has hardened into concepts, metaphors that have become sacrosanct. To these it withdraws as if to a concrete base in order to be able to maintain the impregnability of the natural mind. The concepts that are the metaphors of the day before yesterday, the analogies of yesterday, condemn the

[125] Measure of all things.
[126] Word.

mind of the peoples to its unhistorical mode of thinking in commonplaces—a legacy that may on no account be acknowledged for what it is. The Protestants, even the most radical of biblical critics, believe that they can read their New Testament without the Holy Spirit of the Church, and they read it not with the help of the last two thousand years, but against and without it. Thus the collective mind deals in the same way with time and space. It likes here, too, to forget the standard—that is, the reckoning of time from "the year of our Lord." Just as in space it ends by having nothing above, so it lives out its subjective life without the myth of the reckoning of time, without the profound saying: "If they were not dead, they would still be living today." To this end it has created the vacuum space of concepts with which it fabricates for itself an artistic drop scene for its acrobatics out of petrified and paper linguistic and intellectual properties. If it did not do so, it would have to go raving mad. Because for the natural mind a *regressus in infinitum* unfolds itself; sensing this and trembling, it clings to its concrete base, the intellectual arena, catches on to its own creation, which of course had been planked down by preceding thinkers, much older subjects, but nevertheless just as much highly subjective. Fear for the destruction of the naïve ego, which constitutes its own standards, cheats the natural mind of its mastery over time and space. Here the Logos doctrine of the Savior comes in. The Logos is redeemed from itself, from the curse of always only being able to correct itself by itself. It enters into relationship with the object of knowledge. "The Word became Flesh"—on that proposition *everything* indeed depends. While the word of man must always become a concept and thereby stagnant and degenerate, God speaks to us with the "word become flesh," through the Son. And so the Christian revelation is the healing of the Babylonian confusion of tongues, the bursting open of the prison, but also the sign on the new tongues, speech that is now informed with soul. Since then, it has become worthwhile to think again, because thought has a standard outside itself, in the visible footsteps of God.

Do you now understand why I am so far from finding in Christianity the Judaizing of the pagans? That from which

Christ redeems is exactly the boundless naïve pride of the Jew, which you yourself exhibit. In contrast to the peoples talking the 372 languages of Babel, this pride was and is well founded, and therefore the Jews were separated and chosen out of all the peoples of the earth, until the destruction of the Temple. But Christianity redeems the individual from family and people through the new unity of all sinners, of all who are weary and heavy laden. That is Christianity, and its bond is equal need. My brain is going on strike and I am getting stupid. I only know that I should like to wax eloquent over *peccatum originale*[127] and *superbia judaica*,[128] but the machine has run dry. I am so exhausted that you must make do with this. I feel as though I were always writing the same thing. My love to you. Fortunately you do not know what you do.

Your E. R.

13   *Eugen to Franz*

October 30, 1916

Dear Friend,

I must go on now. It is the question of the un-Jewish life to which the Jew, and the un-Christian life to which the Christian, is condemned. With the Christian, this incurable rift between his actual life, from his froglike point of view, and the *vita illuminata*[129] for which he longs, is the foundation and the cornerstone of his faith. "Let everyone take up his Cross and follow me." A man can become a Christian only if he doesn't indulge in himself. Incidentally, don't imagine that by "worm" and suchlike I am spinning allegories; these things have come into existence in the external world, so that we can now possess and use them as symbols for our inner world, as *significatio*[130] and *explicatio*.[131]

---

[127] Original sin.
[128] The Pride of the Jews.
[129] Blessed, enlightened life.
[130] Inner (and symbolizing) meaning.
[131] Explanation and justification.

So historical facts and the facts of the religious consciousness that are related to them are all equally real. Man goes best on two legs. All revelation is something that gives us a standard, and at the same time it is a sensible, perceptible event; and so for the Kantians it is a *contradictio in adjecto*.[132] The Christian kingdom is thus not of this world, nor is even the kingdom of the Christian priest. His actual un-Christian life here and now is a stumbling block to him, and he is perhaps hard put to it, even to treat himself as his neighbor. But when the Jew *principaliter* and *essentialiter* lives, prays, plays the organ, and thinks in an un-Jewish manner—what then? Jews without the Temple and the Law, without marriage at 18, and without freedom from military service? F.R. as a volunteer in the army? I believe you would if necessary even fight a duel. "Separated from all the peoples of the earth" even if your friend . . . lets his wife go over to Judaism? Where is there the metaphysics of the seed of Abraham? Since A.D. 70 there have only been peoples, and the chosen people has sunk into being a mere coloring reagent in all nations. That very correlation of the development of Jewish thought and Christian philosophy which you described in the Middle Ages carries this implication for me; it is further evidence of the fetters that have enslaved post-messianic Judaism. The teachings and events, which through the continuous stimulus of Christianity have changed the face of the earth during the last thousand years, have as their opposite numbers in Judaism a couple of distinguished names, pressed into the service of the pride of the Synagogue, and otherwise nothing.

Abraham sacrifices his son; in the New Testament he who brings the covenant with God sacrifices himself. That is the whole difference. Among the pagans as with the Jews, everyone aspires to be founder, father, owner, testator, ancestor, guardian, master. Each one rules over a bit of the world. The Christian, on the other hand, knows a second kingdom of poverty, weakness, dependence, minority, shame, repentance, and shy childishness. Abraham sacrifices what he has, Christ what he is.

The Synagogue has been talking for two thousand years about

---

[132] An additional paradox or contradiction.

what she had, because she really has absolutely nothing; but she does not experience and will, therefore, not experience what she is. She portrays the curse of self-assurance, of pride in her nobility, and thoughtless indifference towards the law of growth of the united universe, the "Peace on Earth to all men in whom he is well pleased." That new humanity from universal need and sin, that ever newly born *corpus christianum* of all men of good will—that being called out from all people—is something of which she knows nothing. She knows an original union in blood, that of the chosen people, but no final becoming united of all the children of the Father. The Jews have the saying that one day all people will come to Jerusalem to pray, and they always crucify again the one who came to make the word true. In appearance they wait upon the word of the Lord, but they have grown through and through so far away from revelation that they do everything they can to hinder its reality. With all the power of their being they set themselves against their own promises. They are the image on earth of Lucifer, the highest of the angels, elect of God, who wanted to keep God's gift for himself as a dominion in his own right, and fell. So Israel stands upon its own inalienable right. This naïve way of thinking that one has won inalienable rights in perpetuity against God, which by nature remain for posterity as properties inherited by bequest, is the relic of blind antiquity in Judaism. The pagan tribes cried, διογενής, εὐγενής[133] of themselves. Who believes them? You ought not to say that it is quite unnecessary to believe them, provided that they believed it themselves.

Individuals and peoples ought, that is to say, to live and work freely without fear and without accidental barriers. Just as a people perishes when it can no longer physically defend itself by itself, so every people needs in spiritual things to develop the law of its life, a development that must depend on its own vitality. Every power must stand the test of every danger. Light does not know anything about resignation and capitulation. It penetrates everywhere. It overcomes, and thereby shows what it is.

But I will not allow any *rabies theologica*[134] to come in. I know

[133] Sprung from Zeus, nobly born.
[134] Theological madness.

that Israel will survive all the peoples, but you have no aptitude for theology, for the search for truth, any more than for beauty. Ye shall make for yourselves no graven image. At this cost the eternal Jew is allowed to live. Because he holds on to life in such an unlimited way, it is granted to him. But he is thereby condemned to live by the sweat of his brow and always on credit, always borrowing everything that makes life worth living. The Jew dies for no country and no cause; because he does not experience the boundaries of life he lives by a ghostly reflection of all real life, which is unthinkable without sacrificial death and the nearness of the abyss. In order that Israel may live, the individual Jew depends on his success, on the number of his children. He is a paragraph of the Law. *C'est tout.* You may well believe you have a ship of your own. But you have no idea of the sea or you would not talk like that. You know no shipwreck; you cannot go astray, you see God with constant clarity, and so you need no mediator, who looks at you when you can no longer look out over the edge of the world and are frustrated in failure. You do not know that the world is movement and change. The Christian says there are day and night. You are so moonstruck that you take the sight of night for the only sight there is, and take the minimum of light, the night, for the all-inclusive idea that embraces day and night! *Lasciate ogni speranza; nondum viventes jam renuntiavistis.*[135]

E. R.

14   *Eugen to Franz*

November 2, 1916

Dear R.,

Just now I am copying your last letter in ink in the durability and ἀναγνωστόν[136] of my half-inch handwriting. It had the same

[135] "Renounce all hope, before ye came to life, you already have renounced it." The first three words are taken from Dante (i.e., the inscription upon the gate of the Inferno).
[136] Legibility.

effect on me as the books I used to read during the summer in Leipzig, lying on the sofa, and always threw at the wall because my stomach remonstrated too violently. Man, how you treat History! How you see everything as isolated, as individuals, where I see only the branches of a mighty tree! You arrange things in extraordinary relations and contrasts to one another. The naïveté of a spiritual John, the personal experience of Paul. Gnosticism lays its finger on them, first the substantial and then the formal dogma developed. You are, in fact, Troeltsch *plus* Harnack. The Church of the spirit becomes the Church of tradition and so forth. As an antithesis, you ought to have a little more faith than those archimandrites of naturalism.

Christianity and the Church: the one insures the rebirth of the mystery, the other lives it in individuals. Every Christian experiences the dogmas of the Church as μαρτυύς,[137] as his personal experience. Redemption means precisely that one can appropriate a proposition of Nicaea and Constantinople, such as the *"qui locutus est per prophetas"*[138] as a personal experience and as the highest valid actual truth. The nearer you reach the historical incarnation of God, the fewer the institutional irrelevancies with which the rebirth of the Gospel came among all men whom it reached. Just because those who are born in these latter days ought to be so much more hidden (Kierkegaard's word), redeemed, blessed (the Church's expression), so must there be a much richer outspokenness and expression and presentation of the Gospel. The opposing propositions within the Church are all only *martyria, testimonia fidei,*[139] all in their ways equally naïve and sophisticated. "Nature has neither kernel nor shell, she is everything at the same time."[140] John, this "quite naïve spiritual writer," is in fact both the greatest apologist and the first. Every living thing on earth carries with the power of life at the same time the powers of self-defense, self-preservation, in brief, of protection and discrimination, the *"differentia specifica"*[141] as

[137] Witness.
[138] "Who spoke by means of the prophets."
[139] Witnesses to the faith.
[140] A verse by Goethe.
[141] Specifying difference.

actual forces within itself. In the Church that alone has led to a boundless individualizing, or rather atomizing, which was either only naïve or only sophisticated, or that tried with the head alone to push down the wall of the divine mystery, or with the body alone to taste the sweetness of the mystery. So you have both parties, Mystics and Protestants; within the Church both the Franciscan and the Dominican are possible, which is to say that differences of emphasis between naïve and sophisticated are not unchristian or heretical. Only to divorce them from one another leads to apostasy and death. So the combination of naïve and sophisticated must remain within each individual man; just as every hale and healthy man has two legs, in the same way he must know how to be humble and how to be bold. The Christian Church, the fellowship of the mystery, holds fast within itself these two fundamental powers of the natural man, being willing to be this essential contradiction in terms (cross = church). The personal experience of Paul is valid, the naïveté of John doesn't exist in your sense. The church is the eternal recurrence of the same; Nietzsche divined this fact and had to break out in frenzy. For no individual can bear this as an individual. Without the total conception of the Church, the particular impulses of the first, second, third, fourth, fifth centuries appear only as levers and rods of a steamhammer, pushing backwards and forwards on themselves a thousand times, when you have done justice to a single part, by describing first its substance and, secondly, its function. But in the case of a living spirit this is not enough. Here, that is, there is a third factor, the mystery of the microcosm, the infinity of the individual soul which gives rebirth to the whole macrocosm, though it functions nonetheless as a member of this great body. This possessing of the whole, and yet not possessing it, in the individual is the secret of the Church, and what distinguishes it from all merely objectified forms of mind (Stage, Art, Religion, in the liberal Hegelian sense); for it speaks, and allows the individual as microcosm to speak and to live in the macrocosm, that is to experience consciously (*Erleben* —a word that you don't get in English, French, or Italian) the double mystery of member and of whole as the crux, whereas Law is essentially only lived, Art is essentially only expressed, and Religion, in the Hegelian sense, is, generally speaking, dozed over.

So a *historia specierum et generum naturalia et naturalisans*[142] can arrange a lot of little bags of sweets in order; thesis, antithesis, synthesis, or whatever else you like to make the schematism; and from Moses, Jesus, Paul, Gnosticism, Mohammed, Luther, Robespierre, and Johannes Müller of the Main River[143] spin through the centuries, an apparently magnificent web of Ariadne. Only don't think that that would be a church history with any meaning. As you do not know, and so do not believe, the reason that the Church is in the world, you ought not to confront the "Church of the spirit" with the "Church of tradition" and the "good time" up to Constantine with the "bad time" since Constantine, like the primitive Eduard Schwartz,[144] and put all this forward as "history." He who has no trust in the whole can see nothing but mere bricks,
Valete!

Eugen

15   *Franz to Eugen*

Tuesday, November 7, 1916

Dear E.,

Early today I learnt by experience that rosewood[145] is the hardest wood there is, so that I was forced to think of you, and exactly two hours after your two letters arrived. Yes indeed, here is the real tough Rosenstock, and now I no longer have any difficulty in writing to you. You have given me a much more

[142] A natural history of species and kinds.
[143] A lay evangelist whom Eugen was to discuss in his book *Die Hochzeit des Kriegs und der Revolution* (Würzburg: Patmos Verlag, 1920).
[144] Eduard Schwartz (1858–1940), a classical philologist, who wrote a book on Emperor Constantine and the Christian Church, published in 1913, condemning the Church after Constantine.
[145] *Rosenstock.*

impersonal answer than I asked for. In many ways so impersonal that I asked myself this morning: Haven't I really written all this before, for him to write it to me?

You are quite right in everything you say in your *rabies theologica*. I really mean, you must know that I know all that. And that I also know that you have to see Judaism like that. I was only puzzled that right at the beginning of our correspondence you talked differently from the way in which you do now. Nevertheless, there is a point beyond which neither Christian rabies, nor Jewish Rabulistic should go, however much both would like to do so once they have got into their stride. For you may curse, you may swear, you may scratch yourself as much as you like, you won't get rid of us, we are the louse in your fur. (If only your philosophy of nature were true and it were really its single purpose to give material for parables, and the consequences did not generally go beyond this!) We are the internal foe; don't mix us up with the external one! Our enmity may have to be bitterer than any enmity for the external foe, but all the same—we and you are within the same frontier, in the same Kingdom.[146] That is the mistake in your construction, namely that you fight against Judaism as Paganism, and I can, I believe, make the contents of your two letters revolve round this point, both the letters περὶ τῶν ἔθνων[147] and that περὶ τοῦ Ἰουδαισμοῦ.[148]

Isn't it strange that the ἔθνη[149] have no –ism, while the Ἰουδαῖοι[150] exactly correspond to the ἔθνη; and though the ἔθνη mean for the παιδεία[151] of the world not only a fact, but also an idea, and so you would expect all the more that they would form an –ism? (In Iliad B the Alexandrian scholiast makes this plain, in that Homer counts the barbarians διὰ ἔθνων,[152] and

[146] That is, in the realm of the Spirit the two forms of faith must be both mutually exclusive and complementary. In a poem written by Eugen after this correspondence there occurs the phrase, "Enemies in Space, Brethren in Time."

[147] Concerning the pagans.

[148] Concerning Judaism.

[149] Pagans.

[150] Jews.

[151] Education.

[152] By peoples.

only the Greeks διὰ πόλεων.[153] This, however, does not seem to me sufficiently certain from the text.) Islam was the first to form a historical concept of paganism (Dschahilijjatum), and the nineteenth century formed an –ism for ἔϑνος for the first time, namely, nationalism. But that no longer means what ἐϑνισμός would have meant in the year o, namely, the creation of the idea of Paganism, but the complete Christianizing of the conception of a "people." For nationalism expresses not merely the peoples' belief that they come *from* God (that, as you rightly say, the pagans also believe), but that they go *to* God. But now peoples do have this belief, and hence 1789 is followed by 1914–1917, and yet more "from . . . to's"; and the Christianizing of the concept of a "people" is not yet the Christianizing of the people themselves[154] (of the "circle of the world," as you said, with a queer echo of the language of the translators of the Jewish prayer book).

That is why even today, when the idea of being elected has become a coloring reagent in every nation, the election of the Jews is something unique, because it is the election of the "one people," and even today our peculiar pride or peculiar modesty, the world's hatred or the world's contempt, rejects an actual comparison with other peoples. Though its content has now become something universal, it has lost nothing of its metaphysical weight. (Its atavism was only a symbol, and only Messianism had real meaning for it.) For it still remains, and will always remain, the only visible actual embodiment of the attained goal of unity (the one people on earth, as it calls itself in the Sabbath prayer), whereas the peoples are only on the way to this desired goal, and must be so, if it is indeed ever really to be attained.

For the Jewish idea of election is from the outset anything but naïve. If it had been, you would have been right in comparing it with the race born from Zeus and nurtured by Zeus. But it is not in the least naïve. It discovers its "origin" only when it has learnt about its "destiny." If it were naïve, i.e. atavistic, in its meaning, then hatred of the Jews would be inexplicable, since

[153] By cities.

[154] That is, modern nationalism has provided a secular substitute for the conceptions of Messianism and Election.

one crow does not peck out another's eyes. But on Sinai (not, say, by terebinths of Mamre), so says an old punning legend, Israel has inherited the "sinna," the hatred of the peoples. The Jews are the only *un*-naïve people in antiquity, and so of course Christianity, which takes away from antiquity the ingenuous confidence of its πο$\tilde{v}$ στ$\tilde{\omega}$,[155] is to that extent a "Judaizing of the pagans."

Your description of paganism corresponds, then, notwithstanding the different ways we put it, very much to what I take my own point of view to be. That I was not sure of it may be attributable to the fact that I could not follow what you made of the philosophical background of "language." This has changed in the meantime; now my mind also plays on language in a lively way. But now I should like to explain the idea of the pagans once more, with reference to the idea of the peoples, as you do too, because by always harking back to Israel's being a people, you inadvertently reduce it to the idea of paganism.

Augustine in one passage contrasts his own political philosophy with that of Cicero. I think it is in the book before the last in the City of God (this is a passage, moreover, that, apart from the transformation of chiliastic ideas in the same context, I consider to be the key passage of the whole thing—I take the older interpretation, as against Troeltsch). In one section, now lost, of the *De Republica*, Cicero allotted to the State the two absolute ends of self-preservation and fidelity to contracts, which ends can obviously come into conflict with one another (e.g. Saguntum), and then fidelity must be preferred before safety. Thus in the *civitas terrena*; but in the *civitas Dei*[156] a conflict between faith and salvation is not possible. Here Augustine could have quoted Isaiah 7:9, if the Latin translator had not offered another text (from which the *"credo ut intelligam"*[157] is usually obtained). Luther translates it very finely: "If you do not believe, you do not abide." "To believe" and "to abide" are one and the same. The secularizing of this idea is modern nationalism, which

---

[155] The Archimedean point: "where I stand."
[156] City on earth . . . city of God.
[157] I believe, that I may understand.

becomes imperialism in order to have a good conscience. The defenders of the citadel of Jerusalem hoped up to the last moment for a miracle; not for them was the great, awe-inspiring naïveté of pagan faith, which lives to the end and dies, and asks no more, hopes no more—the impulse that inspired Thermopylae, Carthage, Saguntum. In the world of revelation there is no "abiding" without "believing," because all belief is anchored in an abiding reality; the anchor could hardly have been an ancient symbol of hope, since hope, when present, is autonomous and not anchored.

Now that I want to continue, I find that everything that I want to write is something I can't express to you. For now I would have to show you Judaism from within, that is, to be able to show it to you in a hymn, just as you are able to show me, the outsider, Christianity. And for the very reason that you can do it, I cannot. Christianity has its soul in its externals; Judaism, on the outside, has only its hard protecting shell, and one can speak of its soul only from within. So it can't be done—and you must take my word for it that the, as it were, abstract character of the religious life is the same with us and with you. Beginning and end, if I may so express it, are the same with us and with you; to use Newton as affording a parable, the continually approaching and the continually vanishing curves have the same formula with both of us, and you know that one can define the whole curve from an equation of this kind, but you and we choose different points on the path of the curve in order to describe it, and therein lies our difference. You rightly put your finger on this difference in speaking of Moriah and Golgatha. But you have read your Genesis 22 badly. You have confused Abraham and Agamemnon. The latter indeed sacrificed what he had for the sake of something else that he wanted, or, if you like, that he considered it his duty to want. Indeed, he did not perform the sacrifice himself; he only gave it up, and stood with veiled head close by. But Abraham did not offer something, not "a" child, but his only son, and what is more, the son of the promise, and sacrificed him to the God of this promise (the traditional Jewish commentary reads this paradox into the text); the meaning of the promise according to human understanding becomes impossible through this sacrifice. Not for nothing is this story associated with our highest festivals; it is the prototype of the sacrifice not of one's own person (Golgatha), but of one's existence in one's people, of the "son" and of all future sons (for we base our claims before God on this sacrifice, or rather on this readiness to sacrifice, and it is the sacrifice of the father [not of the son], as is emphasized in the story). The son is given back; he is now only the son of the promise. Nothing else happens, no Ilium falls, only the promise remains firm; the father was ready to sacrifice not for the sake of some Ilium, but for the sake of nothing. Agamemnon sacrifices something "that he had"; Abraham, all that he could be; Christ, all that he is.[158] Yes, that is really, as you say, "the whole difference." To the "naïve" laying claim to an inalienable right before God corresponds, you forget, just as naïve a taking up of a yoke of inalienable sufferings, which we—"naïvely"?—know is laid upon us (cf. the traditional commentary on Isaiah 53) "for the redemption of the world." (Lucifer? Please don't mix up those symbols!) And yet we do not work at this redemption, though it will also mean our redemption from suffering. On the contrary: to the holy restlessness of your work corresponds in us a holy dread that the redemption might not come "before the time" (in which connection there are the most peculiar and even grotesque legends, both old and new)—a dread that forms the metaphysical ground of our relation to Christianity, just as your restlessness forms the ground of your relation to Judaism.

Wednesday

Now to return to the subject: the two sacrifices, that on Moriah and that on Golgatha have this in common, then, as against all pagan sacrifices: that nothing was got out of them (since what was sacrificed is identical with what was given back), but the sacrifice itself becomes in effect the abiding object of faith, and thereby that which abides. That which abides is different; on the one hand, an external community, and on the other an external man—and the consequences of this make mutual under-

[158] Cf. Eugen Rosenstock-Huessy, *The Christian Future* (Harper Torchbook edition, 1966), pp. 182 ff.

standing so difficult that the one side is always being seduced into classifying the other with those that know of nothing abiding. Perhaps the readiest, if not also the most correct, antidote against this error of either side regarding the other as pagans is simply to reflect on our mutual possession of the Book.

Your whole description of the Synagogue since A.D. 70 forgets, or refuses to recognize, that we consciously take upon ourselves "the yoke of the kingdom of heaven," that we pay the price for the sin of pride of non-cooperation, of walking without mediator in the light of God's countenance. We pay subjectively through suffering the consciousness of being shut out, of being alienated, and objectively, in that we are to you the ever-mindful memorial of your incompleteness (for you who live in a church triumphant need a mute servant who cries when you have partaken of God's bread and wine, " δέσποτα, μέμνησο τῶν ἐσχάτων."[159]

I myself have written fully already of how our whole part in the life of the peoples can only be *clam, vi, precario.*[160] No doubt all we can do is hack's work; we must accept the verdict of what people think of us, and we cannot be our own judges (because it is not our own history at which we are working). All very true, and the world draws the consequences, even when some of us (not I) refuse to accept them so far as they are concerned. But that, generally speaking, we should take some sort of passive part in the life of the peoples (and, as time goes on, particularly their Christian life), is inevitable if we are to live at all (and, of course, we always hang on to life "in an unabounded way," but—your legend of the eternal Jew, if you don't falsify it, tells you this— we don't do it from hunger to live, but from duty to live a metaphysical duty: according to your opinion, damnation, according to ours, election. Life has not been given us because we are hungry for life, but hunger for life has been given to us because we must live.) Such participation cannot be avoided even by your

[159] "Master, remember the last things," a play on Herodotus' story of how Xerxes had a servant who stood behind him at table and said, "Master, remember the Athenians."

[160] Secret, perforce, precarious (a formula from Roman law for the invalid and unprotected ways of acquiring possession).

ideal Polish Jew, with his marriage at eighteen (or, better, fourteen and, in earlier times, freedom from military service).

But along with this external life, which is in the deepest sense unethical, goes a pure inner Jewish life in all that serves the maintenance of the people, of its "life" insofar as it is not purchased from without, but must be worked out from within. Here belongs the inner Jewish task of ordering communal life, here Jewish theology, here the art of the Synagogue (yes, its "beauty"!). These phenomena may comprise much that is strange—yet Judaism cannot but assimilate this strange element to itself; it acts like this of its own accord, even when it doesn't in the least want to do so. The prodigious strength of the tradition has this effect on us even when we are in fact unaware of it. The forms of the inner Jewish life are, however, quite distinct from all apparent parallels in civilizations. The art of the Synagogue does not enter into living relation with other art, nor Jewish theology with Christian theology, and so on; but Jewish art and theology, taken together, build up the Jews into a united whole and maintain them in their form of life (which isn't any living movement but just life, plain and simple), and only then do they work as a ferment on Christianity and through it on the world.

How far the Jew takes part in the life of the peoples is something he does not prescribe for himself; they prescribe it for him. For individuals it is very much a question of tact, and even sometimes of conscience (since it is partly a matter of the imponderable relationships of fellowship, and not of duties laid down in black and white by the law). I myself, since you mention it, conduct myself merely dutifully towards the State; I do not take a post in one of its universities, and do not offer myself as a volunteer in the army, but go to the International Red Cross, and leave it when I have the chance of doing so when the State calls up my age group, and I have to say to myself that but for my voluntary service with the Red Cross, I should now be being legally called up by the State. As a matter of course, I wanted simply to allow myself to be put down for militia duties, which would have been the only consistent thing to do, having joined the Red Cross for this very reason; then I allowed myself to register in Kassel for extraneous (and bad) reasons, to enter formally as a "volunteer" in the artillery—which if not an evil deed, was at least an unclean one. I should have done much better by not going to Kassel and letting the whole thing be settled in Berlin. That nevertheless I did go to Kassel was because I thought I would be able to spend my training weeks again with my parents, which would be, so to speak, a consolation for them. I thought that I would be taken into the 83rd or the 167th regiment. I have a deep sense of gratitude towards German culture. If it receives my gifts—poor things but my own—well; if not, it is also well. It would make no difference to me if I had to publish them in perpetual anonymity. The practical outcome is this. I consider what I am now doing to be nothing but "hack's work" in the sense in which I wrote before. But all I want for myself is to see in it proofs of my own capability, and the natural results of my own work, the work in which I live and move in my own personal capacity—even if for a long time the by-products of that work are more voluminous than the products. It does not lie within my power to control this relationship, as I told you in my previous letter. What does lie within my power is only its elucidation, the defining of what is central and what is peripheral; no—I should like to anticipate you in using the bad word—what is soul and what is body. It lies within my power to determine whether I as an individual take upon myself the metaphysical destiny, "the yoke of the Kingdom of Heaven" to which I have been called from my birth; whether I want to live *principaliter* and *essentialiter* as a Jew, even if it isn't possible *consequentialiter* and *accidentialiter*; whether I want to take the natural call up into the sphere of metaphysical choice. The cycle of institutional practices makes it easier to carry out such a resolve. I would not have the courage to take the step for myself, a step that . . . has taken with his larger possession of inherited tradition and (as a Zionist) field of Jewish activity. But "where is there the metaphysics of the seed of Abraham?" I had to smile; if you had to experience this at close quarters as I did, you would have experienced an outbreak of this metaphysics which you would not have anticipated in these particular people. The naïve feeling of the quite "modern Jews" here out-Talmuds the Talmud, and the traditional religious law seems to me (with regard to this border problem) quite consistent in that it must keep open the possibility of proselytism, because of the messianic character of Judaism. According to this the blood relationship is maintained only on account of its symbolic meaning; but the law must rigidly insist that the proselyte only "comes of his own accord," he is not fetched, not "converted," for he is indeed a parable of the proselytized humanity at the "End of the Days" (with regard to this, incidentally, the living religious sense of our common prayers knows almost nothing about "praying in Jerusalem" but only about "prays to Thee alone," and about "entering together into one covenant").

Thursday

So much for "Franz R." I told you last time that it is premature and therefore pointless to speak about him. No doubt you will not believe this F. R., and will treat my letters more and more as descriptions of how I think I ought to live rather than how I actually do. That can scarcely be helped. That was the point of my seafaring similes; if I had meant them in a general sense (as you understood them) I would have been able to describe to you more closely the ship that cannot go astray and whose crew cannot suffer shipwreck; there is only one ship of its kind, it travels on all seas, and its crew only comes on deck at night—you said it quite correctly, it is the Ghost Ship, and up to date—1914, '15, '16—it has not yet found Senta. But the Flying Dutchman will always return to land again, and one day he will find her (Habbakuk 2:4—for he is both "stiff-necked" and "upright" in one person). *Lasciava ogni cosa*—except for—*speranza*.[161] Before the Throne of God the Jew will only be asked one question: Hast thou hoped for the salvation? All further questions —the tradition doesn't say so, but I do—are addressed to you. 'Till then,

Your F. R.

[161] He gave up everything except hope.

November 19, 1916

Dear Franz ben Judah,

So we have chased each other round in a δίωξις ἐν κύκλῳ.[162]
You end at the point where I wanted to begin: saying that I
must and should leave you alone. My dear man, that was just
what gnawed at my heart from the very beginning, whenever I
kept quiet, because I *knew* it. Now me invitem excitavisti in ra-
biem theologicam sollertissimis modis. Me saltem egresso et bac-
chante tu triumpharis et ad statum passionis originalem redeun-
dum esse proclamas.

De ethnicis non totum assentior. Cum enim gentes vivendi,
veniendi, vincendi ratione caruisse recte animadvertas, tantum
abest ut *Graeci* et *Romani* huius mythi vel huius spei eguerint,
ut omnes nationes modernae ab eis dignitatem imperii gentilicii
acceperint et teneant! (Iure igitur Graeci per *urbes* circumscri-
buntur.) Moderna "Natio" idea non populorum antiquitatis, sed
populi Romani hodie imbuitur. Ergo iam Christus vidit et cog-
novit imperium imperatoris huius mundi *iuxta* ethnicos. Nationes
ex vehiculo antiquitatis, id est ex *Sacro Imperio* per medium
aevum *permixtos* acceperunt gladios utriusque iuris. Non *chri-
stianam* rationem vox nationis induit; sed *Romanam* in christiana
ecclesia per saecula gentilicia et dissipata conservatam rei publi-
cae aspirationem et auctoritatem et formam.* So, beside Chris-

---

[162] Pursuit in a circle.

* Now, against my will, you have roused me to theological rabies in a
skillful manner; and when I begin to break out and rave, you triumph
over me, and announce that we must return to our original state of passiv-
ity. I do not quite agree about the pagans. For while the pagans, as you
rightly observe, were devoid of the sense of living, coming, and conquering, so far were the Greeks and Romans from not having had this myth
or this hope, that it is from them that all modern nations have received
and hold their dignity of the pagan empire. (Rightly, therefore, were
the Greeks reckoned by cities.) The modern nation of today, therefore,
is imbued with the idea not of the peoples of antiquity, but of the Roman
people. Therefore Christ saw and recognized the empire of this world
beside the pagans. The nations accepted the combination of the two
swords of the spiritual and temporal jurisdiction through the Middle

tianity and Judaism there stands today a third factor, which has come down from Rome, namely, the imperialism of the nations. They all want to be "imperial" powers. If you charge me with identifying the Judaism of before A.D. 70 with paganism, I charge you with confusing Christianity with the Nations. The Jews appear to me "the" people of antiquity in the sense of being elected. They remained so until the other peoples had formed themselves into the *orbis terrarum*. (Why is it funny when I say "the circle of the earth"? Only because the translators of the Jewish prayer book also knew their Latin.) I could now elaborate the parallels between the years 0 and 1900, and A.D. 70 and 1870, respectively. Today Christianity has a new Old Testament instead of your old one; namely, today its living Old Testament is Church History, the calendar of the Saints and of the Festivals. Christianity now has its pagan "world history" (in the sense of secular history), its Ranke, and in contrast with this its own books of Judges, Kings, Prophets—Councils, popes, Fathers of the Church, etc. in its own possession—i.e. its history of the chosen people. We live in this antiquity of our own, in our own Myth. Today the western world, Europe, for instance, has come to the point (owing to 1789 and 1914) when it can forget the Old Testament, the Greeks, Romans, Jews, and Persians, because it has English, Germans, popes, and so on. And what is worse, my poor ben Judah, it will forget its Old Testament. "The old things are passed away, and all things are become new." Do you believe that Zionism is an accident? Israel's time as the people of the Bible has gone by. The Church—not of course the church triumphant, you heretic, but pretty well the church militant—is today the Synagogue. The epoch of the eternal Jew comes to an end, just as Basque, Celts, etc. come to an end. People have their eras. In place of the eternal Jew comes again a Zion. But that is quite another matter, as you will not deny. If antiquity is the epoch of

---

Ages from this vehicle of antiquity, i.e. from the sacred Empire. The voice of the nation does not assume a Christian reason, but *Roman* aspirations, authority, form, which have been preserved in the Christian Church through the centuries of paganism and dispersion.

Shem, Nam, and Japhet—of peoples—so the period from o to A.D. 1900 is the epoch of chosen kingdoms. Now, perhaps, we are again entering on an epoch of races (white, black, yellow).

But Christ has been so often crucified, proclaimed, believed in, falsified, in these last two thousand years that even this period is mirror enough of him and of the Kingdom of God.

How this will come about in detail is an open question. The Jewish theology from 1180 and the legends from 1600 and 1700 are just as much in the right as St. Thomas and Luther, namely, perfectly in the right. But what about your theology and mine, which could only be in the right again in relation to one another and in contrast with one another? I am not sure whether you are still my theological *alter ego*. But Harnack, Benedict XV, *voilà les adversaires*, as I should rather like to delete myself from the statement of the question that has suddenly become such a serious one.

For some time past, half groping, half by sight, I have sensed the effective Old Testament of today in Church History (the parallels with the Jewish Old Testament are not hard to draw: 606 to 536 equals 1517 to 1564). I am still not quite clear about it. But I beg you, as you begged me, to believe that I am not just throwing these speculations against you *ad hoc*, but it is just because of this that I cannot see you and treat you as my opposite number in so clear-cut a way as seems possible and necessary to you, in the fire of your well-polished dialectic.

You are quite right, then. My earlier silence, my leaving you in peace, did not spring from intimacy and acceptance, but from a real, uncanny discomfort. You want to go not behind Europe and "my" Christianity, but behind "your" Jewish people, as it has mercilessly become, namely, ripe for rest and for the ending of its years of wandering. Put very strongly: No, the stubbornness of the Jews is today no longer a Christian dogma. Christ today has people enough in his church to crucify him! It is not true that the Jew today would crucify him—"they alone in the whole world." For the Jews crucify, judge, condemn no longer! Today there are States and the Church where formerly there were peoples and the Synagogue. Also, there is the law of this

Church, that Christ comes, or rather is there, to fulfill and not to destroy.

God preserves his signs for as long as our blindness needs them. But one must not rely on them, as if they were eternal petrifactions; rather must one hasten to drink from the source, to drain it dry before it *runs* dry. The *Imperium Romanum* its *corpus iuris*, and the Old Testament, both remain only so that they may be allowed to die. I can't help it; I mean both are lying in their final stages, after *tutto tintoretto*, everything has been embraced and colored by them.

You yourself, by the way, taught me this with regard to philosophy, in that for you philosophy is already dead. But what else is the "history of philosophy" but the process of washing out the dye of Greece, just as the "State" is the washing out of the *corpus iuris*. Kant is the last humanist inheritor and scholastic, Hegel the historian, that is, the gravedigger of this struggle of Europe with antiquity. And now? Napoleon and Wilhelm II are forcing the face of Europe, which hitherto only looked back, in the direction of the future, towards the era of continents and the era of races.

The more one excavates Sumerians and Akkadians, the more completely and quickly will Europe forget Moriah, Marathon, Brutus; and, I add, it will be allowed to forget them.

As little as Wilamowitz can rescue classical philology from death, can you rescue Hebrew in its metaphysical sense, especially if and just because it will perhaps once again become a language—that is, a national heritage planted in the soil of a people.

I believe you when you say that you wanted to be in the galley; but you won't find it any longer. You have miscalculated. Don't talk about ships' taverns and of "by-products." *Ce n'est pas vrai*. You have not wasted your time in the harbor, but you have studied navigation and mapped out your journey—precisely in and through those "by-products" of yours. But now you want to get on board and pilot yourself; then you will see—not know, but see, experience—that the ship is already sailing and is about to run aground, just as the ship of the Phaacians was allowed to stand fast after it had finished the fated voyages of wandering

Odysseus; and just as Odysseus at the end of his Greek wanderings went on pilgrimage to a people who knew nothing of seafaring, in order to offer sacrifice and to pray, so the day of the eternal Jew beckons to its close.

That X's Mother was metaphysically beside herself is her own affair; but this was no out-Talmuding the Talmud by modern Jews; that would have been the case only if the son had not lifted up his eyes to a strange woman. But he belongs to the new birth of Jewry. "He experiences the revolution in himself," as you will shortly read in my book (I am quoting in advance). He is the generation of 1914, just as I am; that is, we are the bridge between the world of before and after the war. Not so you; you are the pure generation of after 1914, the youngest of us all. But because you have remained preserved from Zionism and from "neo-Protestantism," you must not overlook the point in the world in which God puts you, in the period after 1789 and 1916. Twist and turn as you like, the emancipation of the Jews is the process of the self-destruction of the European tradition, which has removed the dogma of the stubbornness of the Jews just as it blotted out that of the Christian emperor. (Here, incidentally, the question of Freemasonry and the Jews comes up. Is it really permissible for a strict Jew?) Only today does the saying begin to be valid: "Render unto Caesar the things which are Caesar's and to God the things which are God's."

For only today are these ideas "spiritual" and "clerical" being developed in their purity. The time for mere antitheses has gone by. In reality, the merely abstract splitting of ideas, the thinking in terms of Hegelian antitheses, the arguments between two sides, come to an end. The Trinity, that brazen rock of faith, rightly an everlasting insult to the thinking of all the schools, achieves its triumph over dialectic.[163] Nature, Mind, and Soul are three kingdoms on earth; Christianity has proclaimed this to the peoples from its beginning. Since then they slowly shake themselves free from one misunderstanding after another, from one confusion after another. Christ did not have before him, in

---

[163] Cf. reference to "dialectical thinkers" in Letter No. 10 (p. 103), and see note 174 (p. 147).

the Roman Empire, an imperial power to which one could give what was its own. It was much rather the enemy, a mere force of nature, that slew the Christians. (Incidentally, the killing of the Christians, to me, is one of the most miraculous pages in history: "naturally" you can't understand it at all.) Constantine, Charlemagne, Frederick II, Frederick the Wise, yes, and Henry VIII and Pius IX, are all men who respectively tried to sharpen the two swords. But I must break off here. For this hymn will only annoy you or, perhaps, what would be worse, bore you. But I beg your answer on the essential point. I only want to add this: it is not caprice on the part of present-day theology that makes it use a different Old Testament than before. It *must* do so. As little as Zeus and Wotan are a danger today, so much the more mightily do the ghosts of all the –isms hold sway—*Kultur*, German religion, natural Christianity. We have to speak with them, from them, and against them. Our language prescribes its laws, its data, to us in terms of the thought of our generation. Today one must talk in a post-Goethean, post-Nietzschean manner. That is a serious, even dangerous thing to do, but only the man who dares can speak with tongues. Only the man who entrusts himself to language as God has allowed it to become can be carried along by it so that it "transforms" him and others. There has arisen today, in the place of the Babylonian confusion of tongues, the other problem of "translation"—that is, an attempt to heal the former confusion that only creates new confusion. So Luther, who was so splendidly right as a translator and German interpreter, becomes an evildoer because he allowed Catholicism to go. So today there is this great tension, whether the translation of Christianity, and thereby of the name of Christ, will succeed right down to the last atom of the Fourth Estate. The Middle Ages translated Christianity for the cities, the bishoprics, the communities, in a word for the centers-of-government; the Reformation translated it for the homes-of-the-people. Not in vain did Luther put the married woman in the place of the hated priest, and always extol her. Today, the task is to translate Christianity for the single isolated individual who can be anything: Jew, Christian, Pagan. The Fourth Estate, in the sense of the moral proletariat, did not exist up to 1789, among either Jews or Christians. The fact that Europe has now finally turned towards the idea of chosen kingdoms takes away the meaning of Judaism, of the Jewish house, the only guarantee of the durability of Israel. But enough——

I must tell you about Rickert,[164] whom I listened to for an hour during a two-day leave in Heidelberg, and to whom I spoke afterwards. To put it briefly: He thinks your monograph is too long. He is only allowed to present as much as would fill two proof sheets. He would like to take it if you shorten it. Will you? You know the small format; your manuscript would certainly take up three. He did not enjoy it at all, and kept referring to a discovery about Spinoza, according to which in all editions of the *Tractatus* one line had always fallen out. That, he said, Herr X had given him in praiseworthy brevity . . . .

Dear Franz Rosenzweig, *legaliter*[165] corporal, *cordialiter*[166] a monster, *animaliter*[167] pigheaded, *spiritualiter*[168] through much sin and need and misery not elect, but redeemed: Whether you are working without mediator, nevertheless you remain one of those who are the sons of men, and who want to be so. Everything else is *somnia, figurae, parabolae.*[169]

Do you know the Epistle to the Hebrews? Yes, you know everything better than I do. You would not crucify Jesus of Nazareth—you alone in the wide world. Believe me there.

Eugenes Kakoethes[170]

---

[164] Heinrich Rickert (1863–1936), yet another neo-Kantian, this one the head of the southwest German school of philosophy. The joke in all this was that Franz had discovered the oldest program of German Idealism—and this central discovery was treated by Herr Rickert as though it were a misprint of one line!

[165] Legally.

[166] At heart.

[167] With regard to person.

[168] Spiritually.

[169] Dreams, [mere] forms, parables.

[170] Meaning in Greek: Eugenes=the well-born, Kakoethes=Ill-mannered one.

Saturday

Dear R.,

Your third letter περὶ ἐκκλησίας[172] has arrived. I am now more than ever one who has been unjustly attacked. Can't you find any way at all between complete identity and absolute opposition? You have now reached the presupposition of your second letter, and now interpret what I am writing in light of that. Otherwise you would not so readily fill in all my gaps, all that I have not expressly said, with your opposing ideas. You must believe me when I say that I envy you for the way you put things in your letter of today, as a way of putting them; I haven't expressly formulated these things because I had to presuppose a certain agreement here in order to be able to write you the rest, and indeed naïvely did presuppose it (and as far as I see, quite justifiably; you don't realize that as a result of the course of our relationship I knew more about you than you did about me). Having once presupposed by contrary opposition, my "not knowing, not believing why the Church is there," you should then of course be able to see in the habits and bad habits of my intellectual methods nothing more than public proofs of my depraved outlook. I myself am well aware of the dubious character of my method, and am expecting much from the very experience of having to face you. But that fundamental outlook which you attribute to me doesn't, as a matter of fact, exist. At least it hasn't for years. With regard to Ed. Schwartz' view of the year 313, I am inclined today to go to the other extreme: the bad time came first and then the good time. I am only telling you this so that you can drop that fundamental mistake (*quoad personam*).

My uncertainty over the method of my thinking is due to this: I don't know where "thinking" and where "telling" ought

---

[171] From here on, the order of the letters deviates from the German edition of 1935, thanks to a convincing correction proposed by Mr. Jochanan Bloch to Mrs. Edith Scheinmann (Franz' widow) and accepted by her.

[172] On the Church.

to begin and end, respectively. I often used to think that one ought to "tell" everything (cf. Schelling in the little Reclam volume *Die Weltalter*, in the Einleitung über historische Philosophie).[173] I shall not be clear about it until I have begun. Certainly not here in Macedonia. What disturbs you about my way of treating history, apart from the Macedonian atmosphere, is probably this: you think much more in a direct way with your own head, whereas I have an inclination (I often fear it myself, like Penelope) to shove the whole of history between myself and the problem, and so think with the heads of all the participants in the discussion. Otherwise I should not believe myself (though strangely enough I believe other people when they think directly). Hence the dialogue method that so annoys you.[174] Your method is in a way lyrical (like Pindar): you form a concept of the whole, and then by way of establishing it you add on some historical myths.

Now I should like to tell you what my method appears to me to be. I believe that *there are in the life of each living thing moments, or perhaps only one moment, when it speaks the truth. It may well be, then, that we need say nothing at all about a living thing, but need do no more than watch for the moment when this living thing expresses itself. The dialogue which these mono-*

[173] Introduction to Historical Philosophy.

[174] Eugen annoyed? Perhaps a bit now and then, but certainly not by the "dialogue method," which was then, so to say, in the process of being invented—or at least perfected for their purposes—by the two correspondents. Eugen's annoyance, insofar as it existed, was with dialectic, rather than dialogue, and the latter was an approach that Eugen had himself adopted long before these letters were written (cf. Alexander Altmann's article, elsewhere in this volume, especially p. 30). In this paragraph Franz was conceiving of "dialogue" as *his* thinking "with the heads of all . . . in the discussion," which is not a bad way of thinking but is "dialogical" only to a very limited extent. In the paragraph following, however, his conception of dialogue broadens, somewhat, pointing in the direction of dialogue such as that exemplified by this correspondence *in its entirety*, and the dialogical method espoused in Franz' essay on "The New Thinking," in 1925 (in N. N. Glatzer, *Franz Rosenzweig: His Life and Thought* [New York: Schocken Books, Inc., 1953], pp. 198–201).

logues form between one another I consider to be the whole truth.[175] That they make a dialogue with one another is the great secret of the world, the revealing and revealed secret, yes, the meaning of revelation. This ought not to contradict, but to corroborate, your definition in the first of your last three letters, for they are monologues in the most real sense, namely, acts of confession; and these secret words in one's chamber turn out to be the parliamentary debates of the great day of world history. The reason for this is the unity of mankind, symbolized by the "first day" of the world, worked out and confirmed by the "last day." Now the doubt that I have already indicated obtrudes itself; namely, whether "before" and "after" these dramatic epochs there does not lie an undramatic epoch, or to give it a learned name, a Sphinx; and so "before" you have logic and the philosophy of nature, and "after" the philosophy of civilization and theology. I would push this doubt to one side in that I take the two "befores" as protology, and the two "afters" as eschatology. (Likewise, a corresponding contrast can be suggested, just as Kantianism does between logic and the philosophy of nature on the one hand, ethics and theology on the other, but the comparison is drawn between the second members of the pairs whereas Kantianism draws it between the first.)

These two studies of first and last things, however, are, as their names, or at any rate the second of them, indicate, things which are already and are not still to be made. Thus, after all, they do coincide with the "dramatic" epoch; they themselves are indeed the only true meaning of the epoch. All monologues are only concerned with πρῶτα and ἔσχατα,[176] and it is the true synthesis of first and last things to form the meaning of the

---

[175] Emphasis supplied by Eugen, who later quoted this passage as an epigraph at the head of his *Die Europäischen Revolutionen und der Charakter der Nationen*, 2nd rev. ed. (Stuttgart: W. Kohlhammer, 1951). But do "things" live and speak in ways that require us to listen and respond? Living "creatures," certainly—but *things*? For Eugen this distinction is very definitely *not* a trifling quibble about a matter of "conventional usage."

[176] First and last things.

"middle things," that is, the dialogues of world history. The whole truth is, therefore, actually contained in history ("who can draw it out holds it"). Schelling's first and third ages of the world are therefore being taken up into the second, and the second then obviously becomes nothing but the history of the revelation of the first and third.

So now you will know why I think in individuals (I prefer to say in men), and not in "branches." That every one of these men is the whole is a fundamental truth that I have just now, incidentally, rediscovered in a way surprising to myself; that the whole, namely the first and third ages of the world, the system of philosophy, does not exist except in them (these individual men), insofar as they speak both absolute monologues and yet *the* dialogue. I don't want and naturally cannot (here in Macedonia!) guarantee a trustworthy reproduction of the monologue in that letter; what probably offends you is partly the simple consequence of brevity in exposition. If I had been more circumstantial, I would have limited the possibilities for you to hold the opposite view (and so, for instance, to declare to me: "The personal experience of Paul is valid" and "The naïveté of John does not exist in the sense you give it"). Then your two propositions, which I quote in brackets, would also have appeared explicitly in what I said; that is, they were there implicitly. But what was there about the construction of my ideas that could so have roused you to take up arms? That must still be clarified.

Damn it! We are being moved.

[unsigned]

18 *Eugen to Franz*

November 26, 1916

Dear Franz!

Mackensen has crossed the Danube, Falkenhayn the Alt. If that is possible, why can't we approach each other? Externally I don't expect it of an oriental anti-aircraft battery[177]—but "transcendance" might be possible. Let us therefore translate: yes, it has been your mephistophelian taciturnity from Leipzig and Berlin that still leaves me groping. The whole state of affairs at that time: I as a beast of prey in a show being stared at by you for my lust after raw meat—this asks for some vindication; why should I not at long last turn about and chase the inquisitive starer and by hunting him force him to play with me, according to the prescription: those caught together must hang together.

My circle only disturbs the one who remains outside it. My "*noli turbare circulos meos*"[178] is therefore Weber's *Invitation to the Waltz*.[179] If I then find myself fighting against shadows and puppets, you get a pleasant moral reward out of this suffering injustice, and behind the puppet and Jew's cap at last appears after all the old Adam, I mean to say: Franz Rosenzweig.

My anger is only directed against –logies, –isms, –icians, and the like. You see, these modes of expression, applied to living things, make me feel sick. I haven't the scholastic spirit in me, or anywhere near me, and because of this lack of sympathy, according to the most convincing of all arguments, the *argumentum ad hominen*, I mind it in everyone who pretends to make swimming movements in this school sand pit as though it were fresh, living water—with the one exception of Kant (N.B. the greatest of the Jews). But if I can only translate what I mean, I become more forgiving, because then I no longer need to be personal. For "persons, logics, philosophies, social theories, theories of conduct"—all these irritate your correspondent. "People who reduce things to rational order, take up a definite view or a standpoint, or go along a certain direction"—yes, these I see, hear, believe, keep company with.

Of course, we both mean precisely the same thing. And our

---

[177] "Flak," i.e., *Fliegerabwehrkanonenbatterie*.

[178] Don't disturb my circle!

[179] That is, instead of being left undisturbed, Eugen invites people to join in the fray. "*Invitation to the Waltz*" is an ironical reference to the well-known orchestral piece by C. M. von Weber.

monologues are the most perfect dialogue between "school and home." (In the end we should have a cue for our parts: I talk like the mother of a family and a child at home, but live, *in publico*, in a professorial chair. You are the most private of men, but want only to live on in your children, and you talk comprehensively like an ecumenical council; I don't expect to have children of my own, only pupils, and I talk in such a way that only my partner in a discussion actually understands me.)

So now for your cryptic monologue.[180]

Your Protology:	Eschatology:
Science, Logic	Civilization, Theology

Dear Franz, Your Dominicus[181] wants to present it like this:

The Cross of Reality

Opening Bar ⎫
     ⎬ .   "1916" The Year in a man's life (or: male understanding)

Headstart ⎪
     ⎭ •   Self-consciousness (in your language: phenomenology)

Elaboration

1. Course of the year (of Nature) 3. World Year (of humanity)
2. Course of life (of Man)   4. Church's year (of God)

Do these two schemes fit on to one another or not? This "Fourfold division of Reality," this *crux cogitanda*[182] that can be thought in every moment, and which ought and must be thought, now works itself out up to the last detail. In the course of the year each month is such a cross and falls into: headstart plus four special subjects. January, for instance, has the following four:

---

[180] Eugen's German at this point ("Wahrheitsschleier-macherischen Monologen") is an untranslatable pun on Schleiermacher's *Monologen*. "Schleiermacher" literally means "veil-maker."

[181] This is a pun on Franz' name as derived from Franciscus of Assisi. Franz, who was born on December 25, hated all allusions to any Christian analogy. "Dominicus," as the twin to Saint Francis, rubbed it in a bit.

[182] Literally, a cross to be thought about; figuratively, the most important matter for consideration.

Rebirth New Year	Freedom Epiphany	Language (18 January 1871)	Epoch of the World 28 January (Charlemagne)
(Nature)	(Man)	(History)	(Revelation)

April

Knowledge Humboldt's Day	Doubt Luther in Worms	Facts Kant	Mathematics Gauss

May

Force Break Through von Gorlice	Association Marx	Wealth (*Kultur*) Dürer	Equality St. Paul's Church

August

Home Mobilization	War Lüttich	Fate Frederick the Great	Urge to Create Goethe

September

Map of Peoples (Nations) Sedan Day	World Wisdom (Science) Helmholtz	World History 20 September 1870	World Outlook 25 September 1555 (Religious peace: *cuius regio ...*)

October

Blood rela- tionship Yom Kippur Individuality	Elective Af- finities Discovery of America (World Cit- izenship)	Monarchy Birth of Frederick "the Successor"	Empire Battle of Leipzig

Thus, one finds oneself in every month at this cross, and at a definite step that it indicates and forms, and in this cycle one enters on the four different standpoints. But the steps on their part are, so to speak, distortions that result from overstressing one particular point of view, and their sequence is a course in the spectral analysis of one-sided, human, concrete spiritual bodies.

Thus, to give you examples of this too: *March*, experience. *April*, knowledge. *May*, property. *July*, nature. *August*, will. *September*, perception.

It is just as you say. I always add a few appropriate stories to the myth. And so I am also spreading my menu in front of you here, and am very happy because we mutually understand each other *at bottom*. I can readily believe, however, that to you the scheme will appear very dry and incomprehensible.

The vision of Hegel and Schelling aimed at just what we are seeing today. But don't you see how Hegel's Phenomenology and Schelling's "Ages of the World," owing to the way they are done, achieve just the opposite result? They are both caricatures, nay, contradictions, of the conception of genius from which they originated. Schelling doesn't tell you a story, but he talks *abstractissime* about *ens*[183] and essence and *auctor*[184] (I am reading at the moment that terrible "Bruno"—terrible, that is, in his helpless Scholasticism). If only Schelling had had the courage to tell a story! Then he would not have been able to begin with the Creation but with something known by personal acquaintance, and he could have clarified the unknown by analogies from the known.[185] "Once upon a time there was a King." Yes, everybody knows what a king is. Or, "Once upon a time the world was made." That will do too, because it is only an analogy. But when he is proving the "when" and "why" and "what not," after ten pages one gets fed up and slams the book shut.

Hegel's Phenomenology: The leap from the table of contents, a work of genius, to the fearful digestive process of the elabo-

[183] Being.
[184] Author.
[185] Eugen's *Out of Revolution* (New York: William Morrow & Company, 1938) begins with the Russian Revolution and continues, in reverse chronological order, to the Middle Ages.

ration, in which each pearl turns to dung in the next chapter because the swine greedily devours it—*that* is the real bankruptcy of Hegel's own plan! The reason, in my opinion, is always the confusion of communication and teaching. These books should have become communications, that is to say, they should have appealed to our intuition. But as it is, regard for their own professorial gown made these men of the cloister[186] so anxious that they rejected Hölderlin and kept the cloister as an empty shell for blind chickens.

People often seem to turn into such remarkable halves of their own actual minds. Kant's second half is Rousseau, and he hung him in his room (as its only decoration!) since he said: "Rousseau has brought me back into the right path." "Rousseau proceeds synthetically and begins from the natural man. I proceed analytically and begin from moral man." And while he himself wants to stand metaphysics on its head, just as Kepler and Newton stood physics, yet he compares for his part Rousseau with Newton. *Rousseau* has brought a comparable order into the theory of man's mind! That is to say, he collaborates in all his own work unconsciously with his opposite number, his spiritual better half who, he knows, is at work at the same time. All of Kant's "Critiques" acquire a bright gleam of illumination only if one sees that his vis-à-vis, i.e. Rousseau, doesn't lie in an abandoned corner of his mind but is his equal; nay, as in every proper marriage, his better half.

This half, of whom one secretly dreams, but with whom one cannot treat if one is writing for a school and for school children who have lessons they must learn—this half in Kant's case is there, and consciously there. In Hegel's case, on the other hand, that better half vanished from his mind, which soon settled down and became pharisaical after it had been the ἔρως[187] to which we owe his birth as an original philosopher. But Schelling appears to me to remain in a perpetual confusion between both halves, without being able to come to a decision, and himself not to have

---

[186] That is, the University of Tübingen, formerly a cloister.
[187] Eros.

known properly whether he was living or writing and when he should and would do the one and when the other. He is a hermaphrodite.

So, my dear general counter-irritant, that only serves to push the inflammation into the opposite direction—or, in plain language, I fear we are now as much at one in our views and as far apart in our use of words as we want to be and as we ought to be. But there is still one nut to crack: the invariable religious similarity between Jew and Christian . . . I can't follow you there, unless you only mean it as a hyperbole; namely, if to you

$$A\text{————}B \quad A\frown B$$

are equal just because they both touch the same end points. But the contrast certainly does not consist in the *where*, in the locus of the religious feeling (not one jot or tittle of it shall be destroyed in the New Testament); but over against the calm certainty of the Synagogue we have the perilous, adventurous character of our pattern of life, which tears apart the course of the year and of his own life, lays on the heart of each man his own Sabbath and his own "Four,"[188] his particular cross, absolves him from Cohen's and Kant's "love for the remotest," and leaves him only the love for his neighbor. It sets in the Church's year the reconciliation of this violent disruption of the calendar of the secular year and of one's own inner life, by pointing to the wandering of the Lord on earth as the far distant goal, and also by making the condition that we work out for ourselves through the *vita imitative* this stormy masterful life of "the" man of Christ, in that he himself then lives his year in us. Without this cultivation of the new man, Sunday is merely bourgeois, a mere Old Testament Sabbath for Christians—that is to say, nothing. But here breaks in abruptly that provoking forgiveness of sins, which produces the dramatic movement of the pattern. You can of course say that the Carpathian province of Siebenbürgen is equal to the Wallachian Plain, but have you then achieved any-

[188] That is, the "fourfold calendar of concrete life," see p. 151.

thing? In the same way, it is true that religion is religion, and remains so, and in this sense it is found among Jews and Christians. But put your hand on your heart (for we neither of us like them) and say whether it is not also found among Muslims.

No, in the program, viewed abstractly, there is identity; but, starting from the same point, the opposition between the two religious patterns is bound to become continually sharper as they go forward. The "eternal Jew" has a horizontal two-dimensional interest in religion, and Time is bound up in him, and it is, as it were, always being fulfilled just because it is never fulfilled. The "eternal community" has a vertically directed impulse. Because it strives in every moment to behave as if it were worldwide, because even the individual Christian is almost as the whole body, and the microcosm and the God-man is taken seriously, so its longing turned towards Time, towards the discerning and fulfilling of epochs. But you know better than I do.

If you can get leave in January, we might see each other for a bit, at leisure. Even if I am not the walking stick of Ahasuerus, yet I am your walking——Stock.

19   *Franz to Eugen*

November 30, 1916

Yes, indeed: I have long suspected that you took professors of philosophy too seriously. Now it is a good thing that I should be the innocent cause of your having seen Rickert at close quarters. I can't shorten my book here and I would not if I could. You have unlimited power to do everything, even to offer the book to Meiner . . . I always recognize myself as a southwest German student, however little importance I attach to it today: one must take one's first lessons somewhere, and I did it in Freiburg. I should have preferred Marburg, though in that case I would be as little a Marburger today as I am a Freiburger. But it is no accident that the only good popular book on Kant has come from Marburg, namely, that of Chamberlain,[189] though everyone has struggled for this ἄγαλμα.[190]

Your letter has caused me half a sleepless night, because there was so much in it that I did not understand on first reading, and I do not on principle read anything the second time unless I have understood it. Now I think I have got it, and I want to write at once even if doing so were only in order to make myself read it again.

It is necessary (and you do it) to accept the traditional periods, and to avoid wanting to be "original" like the professors—and like ourselves when we were still professorial. 1789, 1453, (1517), 476, (313)—these are truths, nay, the *essence* of history, just because they are traditions. To present one's own epoch is only possible with permanent reference to this system of co-ordinates of traditional historical truth, and thus only in single cases and in order to solve isolated problems. Also, all rational communication rests on this.

Our present concern is with 1789 (1781, 1794, 1806). You yourself refer to the fact that here I am allowing philosophy—that is to say, Hellenism—to be effaced from the Church. *Mutatis mutandis*[191] the same holds good of "everything else." For instance—I quote myself in order not to go into lengthy details, and yet to make clear the connection with what you wrote—since 1789 the Church has no longer had a relation to the "State," but only to "Society." The reason and meaning is that the Church has entered on its final (and to use Schelling's own expression) Johannine epoch; that is, it has become without substance. Christianity has only now, since then, become a complete miracle; the church as an organization and the church of the Word (the epoch of Peter and, since 1517, of Paul) were still things you could actually grasp through the realities that carried them, namely, the hierarchy and the Bible. But now the Church is

[189] Houston Stewart Chamberlain (1855–1927), the anti-Semitic race theorist, published a book on Kant in 1905.

[190] Glittering prize.

[191] Circumstances alter cases (literally, "when all possible changes have been made").

everything; that is, it is no longer constituted as some particular entity, and it no longer has as its foil a particular reality beyond itself, by which it defines its own particular nature. There is no longer any instituted paganism, nor "Greek" wisdom, nor "Roman" empire: now there is only Christianity. That is what the followers of John's Gospel wanted from the beginning, and yet it did not happen, because wisdom and empire had not yet fulfilled their time (you remember what I wrote the other day about Gnosticism). This is why, as you so rightly say, the earlier real periods, the Church's own history, assume the significance of an Old Testament. Christianity now has the proof of its reality behind it. And the Old Testament is something that will disappear. So you say, and so say I. But why do you not say that it *has* disappeared? I answer, because it has not disappeared, but it *will* disappear so long as this Johannine epoch of Christianity, which began in 1789, endures.

It has disappeared insofar as it is history; since Christianity now has in Church history itself something that has become history. This means that the Old Testament has ceased to be a collection of "types" (the people of God as "type" of the Church), and it will cease to be a collection of prophecies, the more the prophecies as fulfilled are not merely proclaimed but (in the course of the Johannine epoch) become visibly proved. But with these two—Moses and the Prophets—the meaning of the Old Testament is exhausted, whether you read it in a traditional manner or in Wellhausen's manner. What remains, and actually only entered Christianity in 1789, is the naked Jew, without Old Testament. Naturally, he was a phenomenon before too, just as all that has been "since 1789" also happened before; but now he is there alone for himself, and in fact my whole theory which I expounded to you in my preceding letter is valid only "since then." He is no longer a witness of the past (the proof of the truth of Christianity, "Your Majesty, the Jews!");[192] he is now only an offense (the proof of the untruth of Christianity); he is not only "he who will disappear" but also he who will have

[192] The answer given by a pastor whom Frederick the Great had asked for a proof of the truth of Christianity.

158

disappeared only when the proof of the untruth of Christianity can no longer be cited. For this reason it is only now that the Old Testament is in a direct sense *his* Bible, but he himself is still, and only now expressly, the Jew of Christianity.

It would no longer be possible today to propose, as Duns Scotus was still able to do, in order to secure the truth of Romans 11, that after the forcible conversion of the masses a few Jews might be artificially preserved on some remote island, until the fullness of the Gentiles had been gathered in; but one had (out of principle, not from choice—yes indeed, from the spirit of the age) to "emancipate" the Jew, because Christianity now needs the emancipated naked Jew, the Jew of the Jewish problem. And for the same reason, Judaism could now produce the emancipated form of the messianic movement, Zionism, the meaning of which you overestimate throughout. It belongs throughout to the series of messianic movements that are continually being produced in Judaism, all more or less grand self-deceptions, attempts to take the Kingdom of Heaven by force "quickly, in our time," which are necessary to maintain the inner dynamic of life of a people cut off (exiled!) from the life of the world. It is thus seen by Judaism itself in a remarkable parable from Poland that has lately been published.[193] Why did even the wisest teacher of his age fall for the false messiah, Bar Kochba, in the time of Hadrian? The parable is: A sick prince had to be got over the night of the crisis of his illness. But he was too weak to stand the sleeping draught, so the physician suggested that they should give it to him in little doses until he had got through the night. And so it happened. The new Zionist movement is a little dose of this kind, and if you knew it better than you have cause to know it, you would know that the inner history of Zionism (the history of its self-consciousness) is the growing knowledge of its own ultimately unreal nature.

Now I am reading your letter again. I notice that I have an-

[193] The Hassidic parable referred to, which Franz had read in a periodical, was later included in Martin Buber's *Der grosse Maggid und seine Nachfolge* (Frankfurt am Main: Rütten & Loening, 1922), pp. 78–79. It appears in English in the same author's *Tales of the Hasidim* (New York: Schocken Books, Inc., 1947), pp. 98–112.

swered you all through in my own way, except for what must remain unanswered, for which you refer me (and I also refer myself) to a future "seeing and experiencing." You leave me to this future, and so do I myself: that is my means of confidence and of courage; if I could not do this, I would be damned.

To pass to particular points, even at the risk of repetition: not Greeks and Romans; you drop the Greeks yourself later on. The Athanasia of the City is not immortality, but inability to die (cf. Burckhardt). Rome, originally a πόλις,[194] annihilated the πόλις in itself (133 B.C.–A.D. 476), became an empire (800), and remained one until 1806. Then, not through the usurper by tradition (of the eastern Roman empire), Peter the Great, and not through the usurper by personal ambition (revolution), Napoleon I, but through the lawful heir, Francis Emperor of Austria, the empire became an idea, and through Wilhelm II in 1914 a reality in this new sense. I do not identify Christianity with the nations (ἔθνη), but it itself makes the identification with these present-day empires—the Russian one, the "Indian" one created in the fight against Napoleon I, the one founded by the Wilhelms, which extends its protection over Austria. Over against this there is no longer a synagogue, because there is no longer a church, but only a Judaism that also "identifies itself." And so Christianity identifies itself with the empires (the world of today), and Judaism identifies itself with itself (the example— nothing more, but as such a very handy one—is Zionism). So, in this Christian world, which owing to the ever-increasing fulfillment of Johannine universalism becomes more and more devoid of sensible perception and substance, Judaism is the only point of contraction and of limitation and is, thereby, the guarantee of the reality of that Christian world. If it were not so, there would merely be the "empires." Everything must vanish in order to become everything; it alone must remain (it must become itself, identify itself with itself). "We are what we are, but we are Jews," runs the catch of a little Galician song with unsurpassably illogical logic—"but," not "therefore."

Your theology and mine? No, that is a quite unimportant opposition, but so is that of Harnack and Benedict XV. (Especially

[194] City state.

Harnack! You do not see how Christian he is in spite of everything. I read his *Wesen des Christentums*[195] this summer). The much more real opposition is Wilhelm II and Constant d'Etournelles, or Mohammed that so and so, or Rabindranath Tagore, or Troeltsch. (For the last named, rather than Harnack, is the real Antichrist among the theologians, because he speaks of the peoples of the Christian cultural cycle. The upshot would be that he would inquire at the Observatory of New Babel when the great comet was coming, so that he could establish the absolute character of Christianity in temporal terms.)

Sumerians and Akkadians will not neutralize Moriah, Marathon, Butros (as I thought earlier); but that somehow is the essence of revelation, to bring an absolute symbolic ordering to history (cf. your former letter, in which that was very well expressed). Jews, Greeks, and Romans will remain the everlasting contents of history because they are the Ἰουδαῖοι, Ἕλληνες, and Ῥωμαῖοι[196] of Paul. There will always be a classical ideal, to Hermann a Humboldt, to Wilamowitz a Nietzsche; but to Evans, Champollion, Grote, Bopp—no one and nothing. (There must always be a demand for Greek, but not for the arbitrary and bad reasons that I give in the little essay that will already have reached you, but for these reasons; and hence not from teachers of German and history, but from teachers of religion.)

The Jewish home? Today it is Zionism (in so far as it is not a movement, but already an achievement).

Do I know the Epistle to the Hebrews? Yes, and it knows me, I think. Our friendship dates from the middle of August, 1913.[197]

Your F. R.

20 *Eugen to Franz*

[no date]

D. R.! that is to say: Doughty Rival!

Dove's Paralipomena lies on the table before me, and has been

---

[195] What is Christianity?

[196] Jews, Greeks, and Romans.

[197] That is, from the period when Franz was considering baptism.

waiting for three days for me to get a large enough envelope. You know what a nuisance it is to get something like this. Thus, as ever in the case of a sin of omission, I have been cheated of my jest that my "Dove" going to you and yours to me were crossing one another. (Why are mothers so prompt in sending things?) He[198] really speaks as though from the grave. All his contemporaries, including Ranke, could not do anything with these discoveries of his. But we know it all anyhow. Anyway, the owl of Minerva has this peculiar character too;[199] it always only begins to take notice of things when the wit of fresh minds had grasped them anyway. A thousand detours, a thousand wind paths, are needed to bring the shaking old men to the point where youth is standing. So scholarship is not progress or the bearer of progress, but the mark of a substitute for youth, the relation between the generations turned the other way about. In order that the old as they advance may keep pace with what the young see, the perfect tense of "see," that is, "know," is necessary. The old man babbles, shaking his head, that he is surprised ($\theta\alpha\upsilon\mu\acute{\alpha}\zeta\omega\nu$). "Yes," he says, "it is really so, I know it" (that is to say, "it has been seen"), whereas the young man, innocent of logic, as you say, cries in chorus, "Look!" Look moreover at the three voices of the old men, middle-aged men, and boys in Greek poetry. On the whole this observation is probably a mere commonplace. But the ghostly edifice of scholarship for its own sake—about which I have the bad conscience of a heretic—falls down for me if one merely crows three times like a young cock. (For heaven's sake don't pursue the metaphor further and think of the dung heap!)

I suspend my judgment on the idea of the "Peoples' School and National School." Now you—or I, it comes to exactly the same thing—ought to design as a counterblast a Christian (or Jewish) school, or rather a peoples' school that deliberately exposes itself to the risk of its scholars becoming Christians, and so obediently

[198] That is, the historian and editor Dr. Alfred Dove (1844–1916).

[199] Cf. Hegel, *Werke*, vol. VIII, pp. 20–21, at the close of the preface to the *Philosophie des Rechtes*, referring to Philosophy: "The owl of Minerva does not start upon her flight until the evening twilight has begun to fall."

teaches Greek, etc. The tracing out of the natural empire of the mind has been a doubtful success in the case of both of us. Though we always keep the reservation of the other half, the spiritual sword, carefully before our eyes, yet only the one half attains to fullness, articulateness, life. (Cf. *Königshaus und Stämme,* and your "National School."[200] I would be proud to have written that work of yours.)

Tell me, couldn't you represent the other side? Or is the evasive remark about lessons in Jewish religion no more than what it appears to be to the *lector naturalis,*[201] who expects from cleverness—everything, even such inconceivable modesty? What if there is some secret hidden there? Is it that the children of this world are wiser than we in building up the Church's order, and we are wiser in speaking of, working and shaping worldly material? Is it that in order to live one's life one ought to keep silent about what one is and will be? Is there any αἰδώς,[202] the αἰδώς of the spirit, of which one can deprive oneself consciously and deliberately, but do so at the risk of losing real, healthy activity? It is that reality, in order to establish us in our divine likeness, does in fact demand that we direct our consciousness towards something over against it, and direct our love towards our enemy, in order to attain the "identity" for which it makes us thirst? Is it that in order to know oneself one must know one's wife, the absolutely other, and in order to live oneself, one must live among strangers, and experience what is strange? Within the activity of reason itself it would thus be necessary to find the escape from self in this turning to what is opposed to self. I express myself crudely and badly, and by adding more and more I realize I am only making it worse. Perhaps you know straightaway what I mean.

Man, you have often reproached me that I think more to myself than I write down, that I demand of people that they should read my sentences transparently, when there is in fact no light in them. And in just this sense you quote your motto, "The best things you can tell . . ." And just on this point world history takes

---

[200] That is, Franz' "little essay" mentioned in Letter 19.
[201] The unsuspicious reader.
[202] Shame or reticence.

its revenge on you, for this motto is the only part of your book that is a lie. Your whole book is but a triumph of Hölderlin's "On the height of consciousness to evade consciousness";[203] it is a continuous assertion: "The best things cannot be told, and must and ought not to be told." Because of that motto the whole book is sold—skin, hair, and soul—as a topical pamphlet to Diederichs. If you strike out the motto, the soul is set free from this natural world, and if you put down the actual words of Goethe, then you write just as transparently as all the initiated. What will you decide?

Your Eugen

21   *Franz to Eugen*

[no date]

Dear R.,

Our letters are crossing one another in a syncopated fashion. So I want to hold this letter back until your next one comes, so that we may again get into proper step—actually just for the sake of order, as otherwise this kind of correspondence, in which you don't let the other person quite finish his say, is very amusing, because it reminds one of a lively conversation in which one person replies to what the other was just going to say.

To take first the "hard nut," the "identical" religion: I can't remember just what I wrote, but it doesn't matter. You are certainly right that the religious life, when it has become a living reality, that is to say, the religious person (the product, the type the saint, for instance) is something quite different in Jew and Christian, and even a contrast, though a complementary contrast, like a suture of two bones dovetailed together (thus before God they are the same, but before men they are direct contrasts). But behind the images on these two coins is hidden the same metal. The forms of holiness themselves are different, but the final root in the soul—what is one to say in German for "the final root in

---

[203] "Auf dem Höhepunkt des Bewusstseins ihm ausweichen."

the soul"? I only know the word "religion," but take it rather as the opposite, i.e., as the possibility of holiness, and then we can understand one another.

Well then, this religion is a "something in common"; in common, that is, against paganism and "natural religion." This common religion, quite real, is the human aspect of the common objective origin of revelation, also quite real, just as the complementary contrast between their saints is the human aspect of the objective oneness of the two faiths, a oneness determined by a common goal. Hence the common distinction of this religious life from all that stands outside revelation (or puts itself outside). Or, more plainly, for the poet only the contrast is visible, because he depicts things realistically; but that common potentiality also necessarily reveals itself to the thinker. For instance, Heim begins with some thirty pages, which describe what is common, and from then on begins the dovetailed contrast. I think that such will be the method of every systematic presentation that mounts to a crescendo. Contrariwise, I could imagine to myself a drama that begins with a fortissimo contrast of the actual types and ended with their common quality. Just look for a moment at Islam ("hand on heart"). It is, for me, the crucial test. The "good Turk" has more in common with Goethe ("In the purity of our heart," "to give ourselves" "voluntarily" "to the unknown" "in gratitude,"[204] "since Islam means given to God, in Islam live and die we all"[205]) than with either Jew or Christian. He doesn't know, and cannot know, the quite otherworldly attitude of the soul that yet breathes the world with every breath, an attitude that is peculiar to religion within revelation (because only revelation means that overshadowing of the world by another world, which

---

[204] In unsers Busens Reine wogt ein Streben,
 Sich einem Höhern, Reinern, Unbekannten
 Aus Dankbarkeit freiwillig hinzugeben,
 Enträtselnd sich den ewig Ungenannten;
 Wir heissens: fromm sein!
Goethe, "Marienbader Elegie," in *Lyrische Dichtungen*, Weimar, 1814 (Inselverlag edition, vol. II, p. 312).

[205] Wenn Islam Gott ergeben heisst
 In Islam leben und sterben wir alle.
Lyrische und Epische Dichtungen (Inselverlag edition, vol. II, p. 28).

is the objective presupposition of that attitude of the soul). *How* that breathing of the world happens is the great contrast between Jew and Christian, but *that* it happens is their common ground. In Islam you will always find that God and the world always remain perfectly apart, and so either the divine disappears in the world or the world disappears in God. I could prove that for you in great detail. But I shall only go so far: the two halves of the form of the well-known confession of faith stand for the Muslim as in fact two quite distinct halves. God's Being, set out in forty-one dogmas, is not something merely provable, but to know the proof is a duty of faith for every man and woman, and faith based on authority is equal to unbelief. Prophecy, the content of the last nine dogmas (which are actually not about the Prophet, but about the prophets), is a historical fact, which is itself of the content of faith, but is not the living foundation of faith in the first forty-one dogmas. And his modern, fashionable presentation is not a forced interpretation of the original essence of Islam; on the contrary, before I knew of it, I had formed the same picture from the few old sources that I knew. (Cusanus, incidentally, long ago in his *Refutatio Elcorani*, criticized the "There is no God but God" as a mere tautology—Kant's analytic judgment—and the "Mohammed is his Prophet" as a mere communication.)

Only for Jews and Christians exists that firm orientation of the world in space and time; the actual world and actual history exist; North, South, Past, Present exist, and are not "of God" (that is damnably easily said in the Koran, and translated in the *West-Östliche* Divan);[206] but they came of God, ought to become, and only therefore are. When Novalis says in his poem: "if I have only Thee," and when the Jew prays it—different names are addressed in poetry and adored in prayer, but to say "I" and "Thou" in this way, and to bind together "I" and "Thou" by "having"—this only Jew and Christian can do, and no one else. The Muslim doesn't "have" God.

My dear fellow, you have already put your menu before me

---

[206] An anthology of Eastern poetry as translated into German by Goethe.

once before, in July I think it was. Does November stand for Forgetfulness? But to come to the point: I envy you the way you work it out, and above all that you have found such a dynamic form to work out. You philosophize in festival orations, at least in this introductory part. That this is a subjective and arbitrary form, something incidental, literature (or if you will, Life) instead of scholarship, and that the scholarship only comes to light in the actual treatment, is to my mind exactly as it should be. I must already have said that to you in the summer. I too already know my future "form"; it is no less arbitrary, but it is less personal than yours; what I wrote to you a short time ago, namely, the different "-logies" is my question, not my form of answer. But I have not yet the urge, and thus not yet the right, and because that is so, fortunately not yet either the maturity of technical scholarship, to work it out. Except for this last point, namely, that of erudition, I myself cannot do any more now than hold myself in readiness; but that is indeed "everything." Your "Year of the male understanding" (the real one, not its reflection in the course of the year) is still before me (at least I hope so, in fear and joy alike). That arbitrary way of speaking is our own way. Hegel's Phenomenology was really only thought of as an introduction, and Schelling's desire to tell a story meant something different; that is, it was not meant as the forging of an individual way of philosophizing. We recognize the problem of System in the Idealists (the way of philosophizing as the real crux of philosophy), but it doesn't control the form of our philosophy as it does theirs; we don't want to be philosophers when we are philosophizing, but human beings, and so we must bring our philosophy into the form of our humanity. (As Hegel did in the Phenomenology. That which you call "swinish" and notice only in the development of his thought, Goethe had already found in one place in the preface—"the fruit is the refutation of the flower"—and he left off with an outbreak of indignation.)

Kant's finding his other half in Rousseau has remained quite meaningless for the history of philosophy. Instead it created the other Kant, namely, the German type of "Kant," that is to say, the Kant of whom everyone must sometimes think: Kant and

Goethe. (Hegel perhaps belongs to the ten "most important men," but certainly not to the ten "most important Germans." A "people" is not really included in humanity, just as in fact all important concepts are not included in one another—this non-inferential character, so-called irrationality, in the relationship of concepts, is the real ground for the fact that the problems of world history have to be solved by force and so by the Lord of all force. Forgive the digression.)

The biographical foundation for this "and Goethe" of ours was the historical "and Rousseau." This is the Kant whom one can and must read over and over again, even though one has done with him, and rightly so, so far as the history of philosophy is concerned. But one has never had enough of the type, or better the myth "Kant" (it would have been quite impossible to write a book like Chamberlain's about one of Kant's three successors).

Now it is our turn. Your letter has arrived. I had sent you Dove without really knowing what was in it, in spite of careful reading. It is indeed quite satisfactory to find that you find yourself in a similar position. It must be due to the fact that it breaks off just when it ought to come to grips. However, these things usually confuse me rather than enlighten me with regard to what I used to know. Enlightenment generally only comes after some little time, after I have forgotten the details. I underline emphatically[207] all that you say about scholarship. (Why aren't there any superlative forms for verbs in German? That is so nice in Semitic languages!) But, to come back to the point: we are concerned with scholarship, just for this very reason. For "the turning of the hearts of the fathers to the children" is, according to the final verse of the Prophet Maleachi, a final preparation for the last day. Without scholarship each generation would run away from the preceding one, and history would seem to be a discontinuous series (as in fact it really is) and not (as it ought to appear) the parable of a single point, a *nunc stans* (as history really is in the final moment, but thanks to scholarship, as I have said, appears to be already in advance, here and now).

To come now to the main question of your letter. Yes, I

[207] *"Unterschreibissimiere."*

168

could have presented "the other side." It is just as far ready as the *Putzianum*[208] was before I wrote it down, namely, quite ready; it was thought out too at the time, or even somewhat earlier. But it didn't naturally belong in the *Putzianum*, and the part about the Christian religious education was meant perfectly seriously, actually just because it did not contain autobiographical matter which usually stimulates me. So once more I could, I can, and (between ourselves) I will and I want to (and not only "present," but act—tomorrow morning, if the war ends this evening). That is why all you say about it (about working better in $\theta\acute{\alpha}\tau\epsilon\rho\sigma\nu$[209]), is to me only the voice of the tempter, and particularly and in fact completely unexpected from you. To strike down $\alpha\emph{i}\delta\acute{\omega}s$[210] is just what is wanted. We ought not to know any longer whether we are "being and becoming" or "working and acting." One's life in oneself must be so living that without noticing it is already "in another," and one's life in another person must glow as fiercely as if it had not yet been taken out of the fiery furnace of the self. That is the goal, and $\alpha\emph{i}\delta\acute{\omega}s$ is the sign that one is still far from it. (I can say so, since $\alpha\emph{i}\delta\acute{\omega}s$ is more familiar to me than the goal.) And so I could take that motto just as personally as you understand it. Of course, not in that half-baked book, which has dynamic but no soul (there was plenty of strong expiration, but no inspiration, and thanks could only be returned for one of the graces of breathing, namely, for the "if he releases thee again," not for the "if he draws thee again").[211] But actually the motto is meant to apply not to the author but to the subject, to the "You" and so to the teachers who are challenged to come forward. So the motto doesn't stand as a substitute for a "foreword" but as a substitute for an "introduction." And so I stick to it. If you want to write to me about particular matters, please write to me about "The Lan-

[208] Franz' essay, "Volksschule und Reichsschule" (People's School and State School), in *Kleinere Schriften* (Berlin: Schocken Verlag, 1937). The nickname of the essay alludes to that of one of his friends, Victor Ehrenberg, who was called "Putzi."

[209] Another.

[210] Shame.

[211] See Goethe, *Lyrische Dichtungen*, vol. II (Weimar: Inselverlag, 1814), p. 20.

guages."[212] I have, I believe, approached very near to you by strange, empirical, circuitous ways. I certainly wanted to do this, but I just didn't know how to go about it. It is the advantage of simple industry that it carries one towards the goal [. . . .][213] So I hope that is also the case here.

Your F. R.

[212] It was in response to this request from his friend that Eugen composed a lengthy statement on *"Sprachdenken,"* representing a distillation of some of the fruits of his own "speech thinking" since long before the war—indeed, since 1902. This *"Sprachbrief"* ("Speech letter"), written in 1916, proved to be the first draft—and the last one, in all save minor details—of Eugen's *Angewandte Seelenkunde* (Darmstadt: Roether-Verlag, 1924), now reprinted in his *Die Sprache des Menschengeschlechts* (Heidelberg: Verlag Lambert Schneider, 2 vols., 1963–1964), vol. I, pp. 739–810. [Also see: Harold Stahmer's "Introduction" to the Harper Torchbook edition (1966) of Eugen Rosenstock-Huessy, *The Christian Future*, especially pp. xxii–xxvii and xxix–xxxi; and the essay "Biblionomics," in *Eugen Rosenstock-Huessy: Bibliography/Biography* (New York: Four Wells, 1959), pp. 13–25.]

[213] Here the letter becomes illegible.

4

THE EPILOGUE

by Eugen Rosenstock-Huessy

Within a few months of receiving the last of the letters in this volume—that is, the last of Franz' letters dealing largely or entirely with "Judaism and Christianity"—Eugen sent Franz two "litanies" that he (and, as he learned later, Franz) felt put a seal on the dialogue. They are included here, first as preserved in the faithful memory of Franz' first cousin and confidant Gertrud Oppenheim,[1] and then as translated into English.

As to their content, it may be permissible to point out that in 1916 the two men seemed to be, Franz procrastinating, Eugen in a great hurry. Franz, at the age of thirty, had yet to complete his formal studies. Eugen, though younger by two years, was married, had published several books, and was well established at a university. Hence much of the point of the poems may be found in the fact that the respective "delaying" and "hurrying" of the two correspondents seemed now to be on the verge of

---

[1] "Faithful" memory, and astounding memory, as well! Even the author, when asked to prepare the "Letters on Christianity and Judaism" for publication, could remember only two lines of the first poem, and nothing at all of the second. The latter, the longer of the two, was quoted by Franz in a letter (August 17, 1917) to Trudchen Oppenheim "for the defense against the pranks of the military mail," with "explanations in verse."

being reversed. From 1917 onwards Eugen was, so to speak, requested to delay, to postpone, to procrastinate—and he is now eighty; whereas Franz, even before learning that he would live only a few years more, began to act very decisively, founding a family, founding a center of Jewish studies, translating the Bible (in collaboration with his and Eugen's friend Martin Buber), publishing his opus magnum (*The Star of Redemption*), appointing his successor (Rudolf Hallo), writing articles, reviewing books and phonograph recordings, etc., etc.

Thus, the biographies of the two correspondents can best be understood as a junctim, the one provoking the other. That this is so could be documented very fully indeed, but it is doubtful that any amount of documentation could convince modern humanists, so accustomed are they to treat biographical facts in a completely individualistic fashion, of the thesis that two men, Eugen and Franz, exchanged life rhythms in the course of their encounter from 1913 to 1918. The arsenals of modern historiography and biography have not yet developed tools for such an interpretation.

However, this lacuna in the inventory of modern thinking does not impress Eugen very much. After all, the twelve apostles, the four evangelists, St. Francis and St. Dominic, and many, many other groupings represent examples of the interpenetration of "individual" lives. Even Nathaniel Hawthorne and Herman Melville got under each other's skins. *Franz and Eugen did exchange with each other certain fundamentals of their life rhythm, in mutuality*, and—must it be added?—quite unintentionally, in total unconsciousness. Individual purposes or intentions were subordinated to a large extent to a process of re-creation or transformation brought about by a most unwanted, even abhorred, exposure to each other.

I

Eugenius Francisco Salutem

Vielleicht ist jeder gleich:
Gleich vielgestaltig,
Hält er des Wesens Kräfte
Reich gebunden.
Doch blieb es dennoch immer mannigfaltig
Was jeder an dem andern heimgefunden.

Nun seh ich dich wie eine Mauer starren
Zu Schutz und Halt—ich ström' in off'nen Wellen
Doch ist's bei dir vielleicht nur letztes Harren,
Zu dem dir schon der Sinne Knospen schwellen.
Nun schein ich dir ein Schwert, zur Tat geschmiedet,
Und bin doch nur ein schnell verkohltes Feuer—
Ein überhitztes Wasser, das versiedet.
Mein Tag rinnt doppelt schnell und doppelt teuer.
Da bleibt uns nichts als tröstendes Bedenken.
Des Einen Last ist Lust dem andern Wesen;
Wir müssen uns einander schon verschenken:
Du hast's—ich brauch's—so werden wir genesen.

Perhaps each is alike
Equally multiple;
Each holds the wealth of his forces tied in one,
Yet so manifold that the other
May realize part of himself in the other.

Now I see you as a towering wall
For truculent repulse, myself a foaming water.

However, with you it may be just a last delay
Before spring swells all the saps in your senses.
While I who seems a sword bent on sharp action,
Am in fact an overheated kettle, water spent.

My day runs twice as fast, twice as expensive.

One balming thought for comfort may remain:
One's burden is the other's joy;
Hence to each other we may have to lend our being.
One has, one needs: thus, we may convalesce.

II

Item Bund, Alter und Neuer
Freier, Getreuer,
Sünde, Gesundheit,

Hie Rundheit, hie Wundheit,
Zucht hier, dort Züchtigung,
Ghetto, Verflüchtigung,
Kirche und Synagogen,
Naturgesetze und Regenbogen,
Zuchtwahl und doch das All,
Sündenvergebung und Sündenfall:
Jedem von uns beiden das Seine,
Aber er ist damit nicht alleine.
Hat einen Zwilling im andern Lager,
Des eignen Brustteufels leibhaftigen Schwager,
Seinen guten Engel zum Finden der Maasse
Seinen Prügelbengel beim Laufen der Strasse,
Seinen Feind im Raum, seinen Freund in der Zeit,
In den Wellen des Willens gleichartig wiegend,
In den Bildern des Stillens sich rastlos bekriegend.
Die ganze Entfremdung des zeitlichen All,
Sein äusserster Atem und Lebensprall,
Das Alter der Welt und sein Zukunftshoffen,
Wieviel zwischen Leben und Tod ihr noch offen.
Die fernsten Geschlechter im tausendsten Gliede,
Der siebente Himmel im heutigen Liede.
Wir können uns weder lieben noch hassen,
Nicht enger noch weiter zusammenfassen,
Wir müssen uns wundern und weiterreisen
Im sphärenklingend-gesetzlichen Kreisen,
Wir wandeln uns nicht durch Kampf und Bestreiten
Wir werden verwandelt im Wandel der Zeiten.
Wir sind die Zeit, ihr Amboss und Hammer,
Wer erblickt zwischen Amboss und Hammer das Band?
Wer übersetzt sich den Hof in die Kammer?
Dem grossen Vergleicher nur sind wir bekannt.
Das Leben ist eigen und metaphorisch,
Ist Knechtsgestalt und grossinquisitorisch.
Gott ist das Kreuz und der Davidsstern,
Ist Tagesmitte und fernste Fern:
Fanget an, ruf ich; Haltet aus, schweigst du.
Wir werfen und halten Gestalten zu.

Wir sind nie weiter einander entfernt
Als wenn wir ein und das selbe vollbringen,
Und wenn wir uns einstens endgültig verdernt,
Wird unser Wesen zusammen erst klingen.
Lehr mich bewahrend warten, indem du dich sicher entfaltest,
Dass aus der Kraft, der *gesparten* du *Felsenfestes* gestaltest.
Lehr ich dich reichliches Fliessen, weil nur mit *feurigem* Kuss
Sich zu weichem Geniessen zähmt der beruhigte Fluss—
Was dies nun ist? Ein so an uns sich tun,
Dass zwar ein jeder nur sich selber pflegt,
Doch grade durch sein völlig in sich Ruhn
Des andern Herz aufs heftigste erregt:
Concordia discordantium canonum,
Abhängigkeit nicht durch voreinander-prahlen,
Der Zeiten Zwietracht setzt sich in uns um,
Des Christen Himmelreich, des Juden Heiligtum
Sind Eins trotz Zwei als geistgesetzte Zahlen;
Die Menschen wandeln hier wie Klangfiguren,
Ein reiner Ausdruck aller Gotts Naturen.
Mit Brunst und Streit verwirren sie das Klingen
Der Sphärenharmonien, als die sie schwingen.
Heil uns, wenn wir uns nicht in einen Sparren,
Ein Lärvlein, eine Schmeichelei vernarren,
Wenn unsre Bahn, aufstrebend und gesteigert,
Sich jeder Irrung immer strenger weigert!
Und dennoch in der Ferne ein Gesicht
Aufsteigt, dem wir im Geist verbunden bleiben,
Wie zwei Planeten mit verschiedenem Licht
Einhellig ihre Sonnenbahn beschreiben.

The Covenant theme:
Here old, here new,
As free, as loyal,
In sins and in health,
Round about, yet wounded.
Discipleship and discipline.
Ghetto walls, angelic flights.

Churches—Synagogues.
Physic's laws, rainbows flitting,
Selectivity, yet universal,
Perpetual redemption, perpetual fall.
Both of us strive into our own.
But neither acts in this alone;
Has a twin grow up as another grain,
Of his own devil the cousin German,
His good angel in getting perspective
Finding fault with him always when together on the road.
Through all *times* his friend,
In all *places* his foe,
In the wills' whirligig equally spinning,
In the mind's symbols relentless at war.
Oh the total estrangement in the temporal world,
In its ricochets, in its cushion strokes hurled.
The old, old world, and the future all open,
Of lives and graves the endless span,
Of remote generations the thousandth relation,
Yet the seventh heaven in today's proclamation.
Each other we can neither love nor hate,
Neither tighter nor looser our dominion make.
Astounded we are, and must go on,
As the spheres will lawfully utter their tone.
We are not rebuilt by our fights, our debates,
We are reformed as the ages rotate.
Of our own age we are as anvil and hammer.
Who can grasp the bond between anvil and hammer?
Who transforms the courtyard into the chamber?
To Him who saw all, the split overlaps.
Life seems one's own, yet is a metaphor,
Is in servant's shape, and Great Inquisitorial.
God is the cross and is David's star.
He is noon of today, yet away afar.
"Oh begin!" I intone; "No, endure!" your silence conveys.
Never are we farther apart
Than when we tread the same road.
And when, one day, we have lost sight of each other,

Then consonance will permeate us both.
Teach me to wait and to conserve,
While you admit the spirit of unfolding,
So that from pent up strength you may wield the hardest.
I teach you the reckless surrender,
For life's Incipit must be dared by a fiery kiss.
Let me, wild brook, unleash thy tranquil flow.
What is all this? Acting towards ourselves,
So that each cultivates his way to the extreme;
Yet just by centering so completely on his own
Stirs up his alter ego's heart to fervid beat.
"Concordia discordantium canonum"[2]
Interdependence not from mutual boast,
In us the era's discords are metabolized,
The Christian's Realm, the Sanctum of the Jews
Are one, though two as figures of the spirit,
As figures formed from sound, so we take shape,
Pure "inscapes" of God's inborn ways.
By brunt or quarrel, we only would confound
The spheric harmonies which through us swing.
Hail to us when we are not fooled by a loose tile,
A larva, or a flattery.
When our true track, by bending upwards, mounting
Proves immune to our own wills' vagaries.
For, far away, a face keeps rising which keeps us linked
As though two planets, in their differing light,
By concert circumscribe their solar path.

---

[2] Another litany, written shortly before this one, included the lines:
 "Concordia discordantium canonum"
 Das war des Mittelalters ganzer Ruhm.
 [Concordia discordantium canonum
 Had been all the glory of the Middle Ages.]

INDEX

The names of the two correspondents and a number of terms frequently used or alluded to (e.g., Christian, Jew, Church, Synagogue, etc.) have not been listed in this index. These persons and subjects permeate the whole book.

Franciscus, 128, 151 n., 172
Fuchs, Ernst, 14
Fuller, R. Buckminster, 15

George, Stefan, 28
Glatzer, Nahum N., 4 n., 37 n., 147 n.
Glock, C. Y., 12 n.
Gobineau, Comte Josephe de, 107, 115
Goethe, Johann Wolfgang von, 7, 104, 113, 127, 164 ff.
Greeks, 33, 35, 38, 48 n., 66, 91, 100, 131, 139 f., 142, 160 ff.

Hallo, Rudolf, 75, 172
Hamann, J. G., 14 n., 24
Handy, Robert T., 11
Harnack, Adolf von, 46, 121 f., 141, 160 f.
Hawthorne, Nathaniel, 172
Hegel, Georg Wilhelm, 6 ff., 21, 28 f., 33 f., 40, 51 ff., 78, 82 f., 92 ff., 128 f., 142 f., 153 f., 167 f.
Heidegger, Martin, 14, 28
Heim, Karl, 51, 96, 102, 118, 165
Hellenism, 157
Herakleitos, 75
history, 2, 28 f., 33, 45, 50, 66, 147, 166
Hitler, Adolf, 2 f.
Hölderlin, Friedrich, 103 n., 154, 164
Homer, 130
Horneffer, August, 85
Husserl, Edmund, 28

I–Thou, 30, 40, 48 n., 67, 69 n., 166
Idealism, Idealists, 6, 8, 18, 21, 34, 40, 51 f., 93, 118, 167
Isaiah, 132
Islam: see Muslims
Isocrates, 100 f.

Johannine age, 14, 21 ff., 35, 46 f., 66, 157 f., 160

John (Johannes), 100, 110, 114, 127 f.
John XXIII, 9

Kähler, M., 117
Kant, Immanuel, 8, 33, 40, 89, 105, 116, 118, 120, 124, 142, 148, 150, 154 ff., 167 f.
Kantians: see Kant, Immanuel
Kaufmann, Fritz, 4
Kierkegaard, Søren, 29, 51 f., 104, 118, 127
Klabund, 117
König, Eduard, 84, 86, 88, 94, 112
Kösel, Father Josef, 102
Kreisau Circle (Moltke, York, Reichwein, Steltzer, Peters, Einsiedel), 18 f.

Lagarde, Paul Anton de, 115
Lagerlöf, Selma, 73
language: see speech
Lasson, Georg, 81
Leibholz, Sabine, 2 f., 17, 20
Leibniz, Gottfried, 33
Liebermann, Max, 116
Lippert, Peter, 96, 101 f.
Luther, Martin, 99 n., 129, 132, 144

McLuhan, Marshall, 15
Maimonides, 111
Marcion, 110
Mauthner, Fritz, 106 f., 107 n.
Meinecke, Friedrich, 6 f.
Melville, Herman, 172
Messiah, messianism, 47 f., 56, 65 f., 131
Mohammed, 129
Moses, 75, 129, 179, 181, 189
Müller, Johannes, 129
Muslims, 68, 131, 156, 165 f.

Napoléon I, 160
nationalism, 47, 131 f.
nature, 43 f., 117, 119, 127, 143